ELGAR

AND THE
THREE CHOIRS FESTIVAL

Donald Hunt

OSBORNE
HERITAGE

Published by Osborne Books Limited,
Unit 1B Everoak Estate, Bromyard Road,
St Johns, Worcester, WR2 5HN
Tel 01905 748071
www.osbornebooks.co.uk

Printed by the Bath Press, Bath.

British Library Cataloguing in Publication Data
A catalogue record for this book is available from the
British Library.

ISBN 1 872962 76 9

Foreword

E. Wulstan Atkins, MBE

It is with great pleasure that I accept the invitation to write a Foreword for Dr. Donald Hunt's latest book, *Elgar and the Three Choirs Festival*.

Dr. Hunt has shown us in his earlier books, especially in *Samuel Sebastian Wesley*, how important it is to set his subject against the conditions and times in which the composer lived. One of the great strengths of *Elgar and the Three Choirs Festival* is that he has done this again, and has enhanced that strength by copious notes of his authorities and details of the persons involved.

Dr. Hunt's musical experience in Gloucester, in Leeds and the North, and his experience as Conductor-in-Chief of eight of the Worcester meetings of the Three Choirs Festivals, combined with being one of the finest interpreters of Elgar's music, give great authority to his book.

Dr. Hunt has a delightful style which is easy to read and deceptive in one way only, that it disguises his scholarship.

Over recent years a veritable library of books on Elgar has appeared. Dr. Hunt's latest book is a valuable addition, and is one of the very few which are essential reading for all those musicians and Elgar-lovers who desire to learn more about the real Elgar and his music.

E. Wulstan Atkins

Woldingham, Easter 1999

Dedication

To my brother, Maurice,
who first introduced me to the music of Elgar

Contents

Acknowledgements

I should like to thank all those who have helped me in the preparation of this treatise, and especially Wulstan Atkins, who has always given me great encouragement in the project and who has so generously allowed me to quote from his book *The Elgar-Atkins Friendship*. Thanks are also due to Mr Atkins for kindly agreeing to write the Foreword to this book.

I acknowledge with gratitude the assistance of Canon Iain Mackenzie in granting me access to the various programmes and documents in the possession of the Cathedral Library; also Christopher Bennett at the Elgar Birthplace Museum for his diligent research on my behalf, and for providing copies of photographs for the publishers. I am also grateful to the trustees of the Birthplace for allowing these and other documents to be reproduced. Thanks are due to the publishers of those books from where brief quotations have been used, and to those publishers and copyright holders of other quoted material as indicated in the footnotes. I offer an apology to any other copyright owners whose material I have unwittingly infringed. Thanks are also due to *The Times* for permission to reproduce the cover photograph of Elgar conducting the Opening Service of the Three Choirs Festival in Hereford Cathedral in 1933.

I recall with pleasure the relevant conversations I have had over the years with many of those who knew Elgar and were involved with the Three Choirs Festival, and it was a special privilege to experience the invaluable reminiscences of my teacher and mentor, Dr Herbert Sumsion. Others who have stimulated my interest have included Dr Melville Cook, Edgar Day, Dr Herbert Howells and Sir Malcolm Sargent. Indeed I have been very fortunate to have shared so many Elgar experiences with so many distinguished musicians of the past.

I also want to pay tribute to my brother, Maurice, for his enthusiasm in the project, as well as meticulous proof-reading; also to my wife, Jo, who has endured many hours of being a computer widow, as well as giving valuable critical advice through the project.

Finally I want to express my gratitude to Michael Fardon and Jon Moore at Osborne Books for their interest, and for their expert guidance through the assignment.

Donald Hunt

Worcester

March 1999

The Author

Donald Hunt was born at Gloucester, where he became a chorister and pupil assistant to Dr Herbert Sumsion at the Cathedral. After a short period of working in Torquay, he was appointed to the famous Parish Church at Leeds and, while in Yorkshire, became conductor and choir trainer of several famous choirs, such as the Leeds Festival Chorus, the Leeds Philharmonic Society and the Halifax Choral Society. For his work in West Yorkshire – he was also Leeds City Organist, and an academic lecturer at the Leeds College of Music – he was awarded a Doctorate in Music by the University of Leeds.

Dr. Hunt was appointed Organist and Master of the Choristers at Worcester Cathedral in January 1975, a post he held until August 1996. He therefore experienced the Three Choirs Festival as student, assistant organist, occasional chorus singer, and conductor. His booklet, *Festival Memories*, published by Osborne Heritage, sets out these experiences, relating how he inherited the Elgar tradition at first hand through the influence of his teacher, Dr Sumsion.

Dr. Hunt is currently Principal of the Elgar School of Music in Worcester, also continuing his career of conducting, composing, lecturing and adjudicating. He is the artistic director and principal conductor of the revived North Staffordshire Festival, and is also the director of the Elgar Chorale and Camerata of Worcester. He was appointed OBE in the Queen's Birthday Honours List of 1993.

The Three Choirs Festival

The Three Choirs Festival is the popular name for what was known as the annual Music Meeting held in turn at the cathedrals of Gloucester, Hereford and Worcester. The date of the first festival is not known, but reference was made of its existence at Worcester in 1715, and this date is now commonly used as the starting point of the Festival's history.

The original purpose of the festival was the performance of religious music on a festive scale by the combined cathedral choirs with orchestral accompaniment, to be held in late summer or early autumn before the serious business of hunting began, and while the country roads were still passable for horse and carriage – indicating that it was an important event in the social calendar of the city and county nobility and gentry.

Religious surroundings were soon felt to be socially restricting, so secular concerts and other 'grand' events, such as a Festival Ball, were introduced into the programme. From the earliest times there were collections to alleviate the poverty of widows and orphans of the clergy of the three dioceses; the association with this charity continued until quite recently. The other traditional feature still preserved is that of Services sung by the three cathedral choirs, although they were gradually phased out from the responsibilities of the main choral concerts in favour of singers drawn not only from the three cathedral cities, but also from other choral centres around the country. However, since the beginning of the twentieth century the chorus has been drawn almost exclusively from the three counties. Instrumental accompaniment was originally provided by local musicians, but from the 1890s most of the players were recruited from the Queen's Hall Orchestra, which later became the London Symphony Orchestra, who continued an unbroken association with the Festival for over fifty years. Now several orchestras are usually featured, including some from overseas. The Festival has always encouraged the employment of the finest oratorio singers of their time, and in recent times this policy has been extended to include instrumental soloists and chamber ensembles.

Originally almost exclusively devoted to the music of Purcell and Handel, by the middle of the nineteenth century the programmes had expanded to include diverse styles and composers, the choice of works largely dictated by the preferences of the organist of the host cathedral, who was – and still is – the principal conductor and artistic director. Guest conductors were employed from earliest times, especially in performances of their own works, and the Festival has a distinguished record of first performances and British premières.

The strong association with Elgar, and other West Country composers, was a major factor in the Festival's survival during the first part of the twentieth century, but the greatest expansion of its programme and recognition has occurred in the past twenty five years; it now enjoys an international reputation as the oldest and last of the great choral festivals in Europe, although still retaining a unique local atmosphere.

1

The Early Years

'A 3-Choir Festival always upsets me - the twaddle of it, and the mutual admiration . . . I should dearly like to see a clever man get on and upset the little coterie of Three Choirs hacks.'

No, these words were not written by a contemporary observer, but by no less a person than Edward Elgar writing to his friend and publisher, A.J. Jaeger (1860-1909) – of Nimrod fame – in 1898. In the previous year Elgar had composed the *Imperial March* and *The Banner of Saint George* to commemorate Queen Victoria's Diamond Jubilee and, in the year of the above quotation, was engaged in writing his largest work to date, *Caractacus*, which he dedicated to the Queen. He had achieved national status and was reaching the pinnacle of his career, yet he still felt that he was undervalued and of little account to English music; indeed, he even harboured thoughts that the establishment supported a conspiracy to keep him from contributing to a national culture.

All this was typical of the composer's character. He loved his Worcestershire countryside, yet he was all too aware of the blinkered vision of the locals, together with the intrigues of their social ambitions, which he felt was a barrier to their artistic appreciation as well as being a hindrance to his own progress; but he really knew that, in spite of these disadvantages, it was here that he would ultimately triumph, rather than from the supposed glamour and superior influence of the capital. His musical activities were dominated by these doubts, hence the paradox of producing some fine scores for great occasions while secretly feeling that it was all a worthless exercise, for the public failed to appreciate his genius. Of course he was wrong, at least in the wider sphere of national appreciation, but his attitude may well have been fostered by his experiences nearer to home, for, wherever social elements appear to have the same measure of importance as artistic matters, as they did in revered events such as the Three Choirs Festival, it was inevitable that the young composer should feel frustration and resentment, manifesting itself in ill-considered words such as those to Jaeger. So what did the Three Choirs Festival really mean to Elgar, and what did Elgar mean to the Three Choirs?

Perhaps we should begin by reminding ourselves of the musical atmosphere into which Edward was born. Worcester was a small provincial city with a limited amount of cultural activity, except for that which was conducted in the homes of the gentry, the music rooms of the hostelries, or at the Cathedral. Those of us who have enjoyed the vibrant musical life of a cathedral such as Worcester in recent years should remember that these same places were moribund in the extreme in the mid-nineteenth century, with shameful standards of daily worship and very little – if any – extra-mural activities. The provincial cathedral cities had none of the new-found thrills of artistic expression that would have been encountered in, for instance, the industrial centres of the North of England.

The great exception for Worcester was that, in common with Gloucester and Hereford, it had the Three Choirs Festival. Even the most dilatory of cathedral organists would be galvanised into action by this triennial event, however poor his artistic talents might be, and it should be remembered that, outside London and the Universities, cathedral musicians were generally homespun and lacking formal training. Of course there were exceptions, like the peripatetic S.S. Wesley (1810-76), but Worcester's William Done (1815-95), who occupied the organ seat for fifty-one-years (nearly forty of which coincided with Elgar's early years), was a local musician of modest attainment – and he was better than most! It was to his great credit that he planned some imaginative programmes for Worcester Festivals during his tenure of office; also, with increasing experience he appeared to gain stature as a conductor. The *Musical Times* wrote that 'the general performances under his direction[1] were very far above the average.'

Elgar was born within the shadow of the Three Choirs Festival, spending his early years under the considerable influence of Done and his music, and feeling the physical domination of the Cathedral, which from a religious point of view was an alien world to him. However, his father's dependence on the Cathedral as a musical centre of sorts did present the young Elgar with opportunities of absorbing the atmosphere of the place, as well as experiencing at first hand the heritage of church and choral music, notwithstanding the poor standards which must have prevailed at that time. It is interesting to conjecture whether his dislike of the music of Tudor composers, especially William Byrd, was the result of inadequate performances that he had heard. Another valuable aid to Elgar's development was the Cathedral Library, where he was given access to peruse the vast collection of musical scores.

Looking down the High Street, Worcester, towards the Cathedral.
The Elgar music shop is the third on the left.

Dr. William Done

Of course the 1860 and 1863 Festivals would have meant little to Edward, except perhaps an awareness of unaccustomed activity and bustle around the streets and in his home for, apart from an increase of customers to their music shop, his family were enthusiastically involved in the Festivals. A little boy who could recall playing in the gardens of Broadheath, even though the family left there before he was two years of age, would almost certainly remember something of Festival times, for these were very special events indeed in the musical life of a city that was largely somnolent in the intervening years between festivals.

The first Festival to attain real significance in Edward's life was 1866, when he was nine. Only days before the Festival he had suffered the loss of his younger brother Jo (1859-66) who, because of his precocious talent, was referred to as Beethoven by the family. In order to take Edward's mind away from the family tragedy, his father arranged for him to attend a rehearsal in the Cathedral. The orchestra, largely made up of local professionals, included his father in the second violins and his uncle Henry among the violas. The work being rehearsed was Beethoven's *Mass in C* (or *Service in C* as it then was called, so as not to offend the sensibilities of narrow-minded clergy and committee members), and the impact of this work was immediate and overwhelming. His friend, Hubert Leicester (1855-1939), recalled seeing Edward running down the High Street with a large score under his arm. . . . 'he had never heard a big band until then, and it was such a revelation to him that he said:

> Oh, my, I had no idea what a big band was like. Then I
> began to think how much more could be made out of it than
> they were making. . . . if I had that orchestra under my own

control and given a free hand I could make it play just whatever I liked.

Perhaps unlikely phraseology for a nine-year old, but there is no doubting the message: Edward's orchestral imagination had been fired by this first experience, and in this respect he was never to look back. This single happening was almost certainly the catalyst to create the greatest manipulator of orchestral colour that British music has ever known. The size and colour of the orchestra was to be the prime factor in the little boy's ambitions. The choir did not seem so important to him at this stage, but the potential of choral sonorities would not have escaped his acute aural perception. He later said that ' historians will decide if larger works demanded larger orchestras, or larger orchestras demanded larger works . . . it will be worth discovering which force was the moving power.'[2]

The first experience of Beethoven's writing was obviously so significant in Edward's musical upbringing. We talk so much of his influence on the Festival; here is the first direct evidence of the Festival's influence on him. Also, is it not significant that the work which probably changed his life was by Beethoven? The Elgar family's own little Beethoven would never appear – except perhaps, who knows, in the form of the unfancied Edward.

The young Elgar was receiving basic tuition on the piano and the violin, was acquiring skills on the organ from being in attendance at Services with his father[3], and was absorbing a great deal of other musical awareness from studying and listening. By 1869 he was fully informed of the Festival's significance, and it is said that it was here that his particular interest in the violin was kindled. The Elgar shop had supplied the orchestral parts for Handel's *Messiah*, which was traditionally performed at the festivals. On the strength of this the young Elgar gained admission to a rehearsal of the oratorio, and was immediately captivated by the violin obbligato to the aria *O thou that tellest*, so much so that he went home and learnt to play it. It took him a fortnight to achieve this, but, bearing in mind his limited technique, it was a remarkable accomplishment, for this agile passage is far from easy. We are not aware of the twelve-year old hearing anything else at this Festival, although in later years he always spoke warmly of his first experiences of Mendelssohn's *Elijah*, and this work had been given at every Festival[4] since Gloucester in 1847, a year after it had first been heard at Birmingham. He might also have heard the première of the first major work by Arthur Sullivan (1842-1900) – the cantata *The Prodigal Son*.

Edward was eventually to play the instrument for which he had found new delights at the Festival for fifteen years, yet there were to be two more festivals at Worcester before he actually found himself in the ranks of performers. 1872 was the time of his transition from being a solicitor's clerk to a full-time musician. Apparently his employer gave him leave of absence in order to attend the Festival but, although the composer frequently made references to the event later in his life, there is little evidence that the fifteen-year old, who had recently left school, found anything particularly striking in the programme. Yet there is no doubt that he would have soaked up the atmosphere, and the concerts would have provided him with additional experience of choral/orchestral colouring and sonorities, where his particular genius would ultimately be displayed.

There was no Worcester Festival in 1875. This was the year of the so-called Mock Festival, when the Worcester clergy bowed to the demands and perceived wealth of Lord Dudley, who decreed that he would not donate to the restoration appeal if a Festival, deemed to be too secular and commercial, was held. The city was in mourning, and its citizens took a poor view of the Dean and Chapter's intransigence. Elgar noted that it was a 'gloomy week', and took some pleasure from the fact that it rained continuously during this 'Festival', which consisted of 'special' Cathedral Services, and no more. One bright spot for Elgar was to listen to the playing of the great S.S. Wesley[5], then in the last year of his life. His playing, and the music that he played, made a lasting impression on the eighteen-year-old Elgar, who was particularly impressed with Wesley's own cantata-anthem *Let us lift up our heart.* This fine piece has some memorable moments, not least in the extensive aria for bass solo, where a beautiful falling phrase and subtle twist of harmony bears a striking resemblance to one of the principal themes of *The Kingdom*. Could it be possible that the much-maligned Wesley was an unlikely influence over the impressionable young composer? Elgar was to return to this music for one of his last offerings to the Festival, orchestrating the anthem at Sir Ivor Atkins' request for Worcester in 1923. It is hard to accept that the score and parts of this work appear to have been lost – a piece of unforgivable inefficiency on someone's part.

Worcester Festival returned to normality in 1878. Among the participants was E.W. Elgar in the second violins, alongside his father, and for this first professional engagement at a festival he was paid the princely sum of £4. Uncle Henry was still a member of the viola section and, to complete the family participation, his sister Pollie was a soprano in the chorus. The often-told story of how the young Elgar, in his thirst for knowledge and compositional discipline, undertook a work project of writing a symphony to the model of Mozart's *Symphony in G minor (No. 40)*, had an interesting sequel at this Festival, for the work was included in the programme. Elgar literally experienced inside knowledge of the work from his back desk of the violins, which prompted him to renew the possibility of taking up the project once again. A second sketchbook was started during the Festival rehearsals, setting out his own symphony in full score. Only a few bars were written, and he never returned to it again, but his enthusiasm for Mozart and this particular work never diminished. As he remarked often enough: 'Mozart is the musician from whom everyone should learn form.' Years later he described the Symphony as 'amongst the noblest achievements in Art.'[6]

The Festival programme contained most of the expected 'warhorses' such as *Creation, Elijah, Hymn of Praise, Messiah* and Spohr's *The Last Judgement*. I wonder how contemporary audiences would view a programme which included all of these major works? I rather suspect that there would probably be an unprecedented demand for tickets! In the 1878 programme there were also some new pieces by Sterndale Bennett (1816-75) – *The May Queen* and Dr Philip Armes (1836-1908) of Durham – *Hezekiah*, neither of which were hardly representative of the best that British music could offer to the flourishing choral movement in this country. It is not difficult to imagine the frustration of a young ambitious composer having to endure the rigours of working at such inconsequential compositions. His predictable reaction, if unexpectedly polite, was put into words later in his life:[7]

> We had been accustomed to perform compositions by Sir Frederick Ouseley, Dr Philip Armes and others of the organists and professors of music who furnished meritorious works for festivals, but they lacked the feeling for orchestral effect and elasticity in instrumentation so

obvious in the works of French, Italian and German composers.

Elgar's suspicion and eventual dislike of academic musicians showed itself at an early age, and was heightened by his practical involvement in their music. His acquaintance with these feeble works (although not all were bad) would ultimately be to the benefit of British choral music. If only for these rather negative reasons, the Three Choirs Festival was steadily making its influence felt on the young composer. When his turn came, as surely it would, things must be different.

Another surprising story emanates from that Festival of the impressionable young Elgar showing affection for the personality and respect for the 'charming' music of Sir John Stainer (1840-1901), now so much denigrated in assessments of British Music of the last century. Perhaps Elgar experienced something in this composer's musical personality that has escaped those who so readily brush his efforts under the carpet?

Yet in some ways the sort of music mentioned above was creating the backcloth on which the Three Choirs Festival would develop, and on which Elgar would quite soon make a lasting impression. The prestige of the festival was improving, as were the performances, although how the latter measures against contemporary standards is almost impossible to assess. The year 1880 has been marked as a watershed for English music, the work designated to herald this renaissance being *Prometheus Unbound* by Hubert Parry (1848-1918), an interesting work first performed at the Gloucester Festival of that year. It cannot be denied that there was evidence of a new spirit around: a greater determination and responsibility was shown by composers, together with a deeper understanding of our musical heritage, not least in association with literary achievements. At this point in time there was little suggestion that a young Worcester musician would ever be a part of that renaissance, leave alone in time become the uncrowned king of the new movement.

2

The Emerging Years

'It was one of Edward Elgar's peculiarities never to speak,
even in the early days, of the teaching and playing by which
he really earned his living . . . Although the Genius was
returning from Munich to play in the orchestra of the Three
Choirs Festival at Worcester, he did not once mention it
during the holiday.'[8]

Perhaps it is not surprising that Elgar did not look forward to the
Festival, for he would again have to experience the disappointments
of his own chosen career, which would be brought home to him when
taking part in the performances of so many inferior works. He was
convinced that he would become a significant composer but, as yet, there
was no conclusive proof that he had the necessary talent.

The Worcester Festival of 1881 witnessed a major change in the
concert arrangements, for the platform was erected at the west end of the
Nave, where it has been sited ever since. Apart from the obvious
advantage in terms of acoustic, it also provided more visual comfort for
performers and audience alike, even if the latter had to turn sideways to

achieve the full benefit.[9] That Festival also saw the promotion of Edward Elgar to the first violins, albeit to the last desk, while his father still sojourned in the nether regions of the seconds.

The programme contained the usual fare, together with some novelties, but the work that stood out in Elgar's memory was the cantata *The Bride* by Alexander Mackenzie (1847-1935). He was particularly taken with the composer's mastery of orchestration, writing:

> The work gave the orchestral players a real lift and widened the outlook of the old-fashioned professor considerably.[10]

The Widow of Nain, a work by a local composer, Alfred Caldicott, (1842-97) was one of the trifles offered at that Festival, but it did provide an early indication of the orchestral scoring potential of the young Elgar for, following an urgent request, he immediately wrote out a harp part for the performance. It is interesting to recall that the harp features prominently in almost all of Elgar's major compositions.

It was certainly a hard week's work for all concerned, and there is a warning note sounded in the *Annals of the Three Choirs*, which states:

> Monday was, as usual, given up to rehearsals from 9.45 a.m to 11 p.m., when the band, chorus and soloists retired to their well-earned and much-needed rest. It was generally admitted on all sides that more rehearsals were needed, one day being totally inadequate for rehearsing more than a quarter of the week's work.[11]

The warning went unheeded, and this rehearsal monstrosity prevailed in a similar form for the whole of Elgar's association with the Festival; indeed the pattern did not substantially change until the 1950s.

If the 1881 Festival had been something of a non-event (and the records suggest that in general the performances were mediocre), Worcester 1884 proved to be a very significant event, not least for Elgar who, for the first time, was to come under the direct influence of one of Europe's leading composers – Antonín Dvořák (1841-1904). Interestingly, it was the Dean and Chapter – presumably to mark the 800th celebrations of the Cathedral – and not the festival committee that had engaged the services of this international 'star' who, at the age of forty three, was reaching the peak of his powers and reputation. To the young Elgar, gradually moving up the ranks of the first violins in the Festival 'Band', it was a profound experience to play under the hypnotic presence of the great man, and to glean knowledge of his mastery of instrumentation from within the orchestra. Writing to a friend, Elgar expressed his admiration in the following words:

> I wish you could hear Dvořák's music. It is simply ravishing, so tuneful and clever, and the orchestration is wonderful; no matter how few instruments he uses it never sounds thin. I cannot describe it; it must be heard.[12]

This is surely a reflection of our own feelings about Elgar's use of instruments. Much has been said and written about the influence of Brahms and especially Wagner on Elgar's music, but when we consider the combination of romantic outpouring and melodic subtlety, rhythmic vitality and contrast, and that intangible portrayal of the countryside (so hard to define, yet so clearly expressed), surely Dvořák is a stronger influence: the fact that this influence stems from a Three Choirs Festival is a remarkable happening, and not often recognised. And there were other significant similarities between the established Dvořák and the ambitious Elgar: their humble origins as sons of tradesmen, their Catholic upbringing and involvement in formal acts of worship, their early struggles, their love of nature, their awareness of a national cultural awakening, their participation in local music making, their natural talents primarily as violinists – but also showing ability at the keyboard, family opposition to their musical career, and – perhaps, most important of all – their opportunity of learning the skills of instrumentation by participation in orchestras. One major difference was in personality, for Dvořák's mild, easy-going manner, was not really a feature of Elgar's character.

The pieces that created the artistic stirring in the younger composer's mind at that Festival were the Slavonic-style *Stabat Mater*, (second performance in England), which used to be so much in vogue, but is rarely heard these days, and the wonderful *Symphony in D* (now listed as number six), which had been completed in 1880, and given its London première during the composer's first visit to these shores earlier in 1884. At Worcester the Symphony was 'relegated' to the Public Hall, one supposes because it contained a peasant dance, and therefore not suitable for hallowed surroundings. In a typically protracted programme of miscellaneous items so loved by the Victorians the programme book simply describes the auspicious occasion as:

Symphony in D   Dvorak

conducted by the composer

There were no notes, nor even details of the movements; but at least the public were able to show their appreciation to the composer, as related in one of the reviews of the occasion:

> On his entry into the orchestra, the applause was so overwhelming that it was many minutes before he was allowed to give the signal for commencing; a similar demonstration followed at the end of each movement, and at the end of the work he received such an ovation as we trust will convince him that English people are ever ready to recognise and give welcome to the highest representative men in art, whatever may be the country of their birth.[13]

It is hoped that Dvořák did not recognise the superior tone of the last phrase! What is certain is that his presence at this august festival gave it the credibility that it was fast losing, and the fact that Elgar, at his most impressionable, was there to witness it, probably had more to do with his determination to become a comparably great composer than we shall ever know. It is certainly not too difficult for the musical detective to find similarities of Dvořák's scoring and structure in Elgar's later large-scale orchestral works (for example, compare the slow movement of Dvořák's Symphony in D with that of Elgar's *First Symphony*), and the colourful deployment of instruments shines through both composers' creations: not a note is wasted. Interestingly, there is no evidence that Elgar actually met Dvořák at this Festival: his admiration had to be contained from a distance.

There was certainly little else in the 1884 Festival to excite Elgar's interest, and by all accounts the other performances were again lacking quality, the chorus being especially poor.

Elgar's frustrations were increasing. After another three years had elapsed and Worcester Festival had come round again, he was still little further forward in fulfilling his ambitions to become a recognised composer, and the 1887 programme would have done little to lift his spirits. Following the distinction that Dvořák's presence had given to the previous Worcester event, the fare must have seemed very ordinary. Some interest centred around the performance of Sullivan's *Golden Legend*, which had been given its first performance at the Leeds Festival of the previous year.

The concert was given at the Public Hall and the chorus was composed entirely of the Leeds contingent of the Festival Choir[14] and, to quote the Annals:

> their rendering of the choruses is acknowledged to have
> been a very pattern of what chorus-singing should be.

We can be sure that Elgar, playing in the accompanying orchestra, would have noted these choral skills and special sonorities obtained by the northern choir, and this would surely be in his mind when he wrote *Caractacus* for a Leeds Festival commission in 1898. *Messiah, Elijah, The Last Judgement* and Gounod's *Redemption* were in the programme once again, and we are told that *Hymn of Praise* 'went as it should go'!

The last-named was paired with the première of the oratorio *Ruth* by the much-fêted British composer, Frederic Cowen (1852-1935). How irksome it must have been for Elgar to find himself sitting at the feet of someone who was only five years his senior, who had already written symphonies, and was hailed as a great choral composer. Cowen was one of a group of British composers who were household names, mainly by virtue of their offerings to the insatiable appetite of the choralists; the Old Testament was stripped bare of suitable subjects in the endless search for new texts for cantatas, most of which turned out to be banal in the extreme. Elgar's thoughts on Cowen's music are not known, but in later years he would have cause to be grateful to the older man, who became a champion of his music. Cowen later remarked that he little knew then of the genius who was under the guidance of his baton.

Yet how could Elgar, now thirty years of age, make an impression on the Festival committee to recognise him as a composer? He had talent to burn, but no one was making any use of it.

Up to that point his total output of compositions had been restricted to works for local consumption: a few salon pieces, some songs, and a collection of miniatures for use at St George's Church – superior miniatures, it is true, but there was nothing to prove that he would be able to write anything of substance. Most of his attempts on a larger canvas had been lost or destroyed. But things were about to happen.

In September 1888 Elgar became engaged to one of his pupils, Caroline Alice Roberts (1848-1920), the daughter of a late Major-General in the Indian Army. They were married in the following May, and almost immediately the local musician had assumed an air of respectability in the eyes of the locals, for the Roberts family were much-respected in county circles. This change of attitude towards the promising local composer clearly filtered through to the Festival committee when they met to plan the 1890 Festival, for the ageing William Done was persuaded to invite Elgar to write an orchestral work for the forthcoming event. Elgar had sent to Done for perusal a copy of the newly-published *Salut d'amour*, his most celebrated piece to date, which he had written to mark his engagement to Alice. He received the following reply:

College Green, Worcester

Jany. 1st 1890

Dear Mr Elgar,

Thank you very much for your kind letter, and for your good wishes of the season. I shall be very much pleased to receive the score of your new composition (it will probably come tomorrow) and I shall study it with much pleasure as the work of one whose talent I have always recognised and admired. It will be a pleasure to you to know that the proposal to introduce your orchestral piece at the Festival will meet with no opposition. I must not take the credit of it to myself - as it scarcely required a word of recommendation from me. I will take care to give you a good Orchestra and fair opportunity of rehearsal. Will you kindly tell me whether any extra instruments will be required. I hope not, as the orchestra is so small.

With kindest regards and best wishes,

Believe me, Dear Mr. Elgar,

Yours very faithfully,

W. Done

The outcome of this letter was the *Overture 'Froissart'*.

The Elgars were now living in London in an attempt to rid themselves of their provincial image, and in the hope of bringing Edward's name before the capital's influential musical public; but it was still smaller-scale works that dominated the composer's creative output.

Indeed, the above letter had been received at the time that Elgar was finishing his *Vesper Voluntaries*, a collection of attractive miniatures for organ. The demand for a major orchestral work was a huge and challenging step forward for one who so far had not ventured into the realms of an extended composition, but even a person with Elgar's in-built pessimism and suspicion must have felt a sense of elation at this encouraging gesture from the local committee.

With time on their hands the Elgars took full advantage of the London concert scene, showing a special interest in opera, having attended several performances of Wagner's *Die Meistersinger von Nürnberg*. The stature and thematic development of Wagner's Overture to this opera would have been very much in Edward's mind as he set to work on his own new composition, but too much emphasis should not be placed on the comparison of themes, as expounded by some biographers, as this tends to take attention away from the subtlety of highly original material by Elgar.

The Elgar diary for 25th May, 1890, states: 'Commenced *Froissart*.' Jean Froissart, a French romantic chronicler of the 14th century, was the inspiration for the Overture, for it is generally supposed that Elgar adopted the title from having been moved by a passage from Sir Walter Scott's *Old Mortality*, in which the heroic figure John Graham of Claverhouse quotes from Froissart to incite chivalry among his followers:

> . . . with what true chivalrous feeling he confines his beautiful expressions of sorrow to the death of the gallant and high-bred knight, of whom it was a pity to see fall, such was his loyalty to his king, pure faith to his religion, hardihood towards his enemy, and fidelity to his lady-love!

Title page of the Overture 'Froissart'

The opening of the Overture 'Froissart'
– from the original full score

This was the sort of language likely to appeal to the aspiring young composer, who projected his personality even more by the quotation from Keats that prefaces the score:

> When chivalry lifted up her lance on high.

The arresting opening of the Overture immediately sets the pattern of this heroic vision, and there follows a succession of memorable tunes, with a particularly haunting melody in the middle of the piece. The overall effect is probably fragmentary as the inexperienced composer strives to formulate a satisfying development of all this promising material and, as Elgar himself confessed, it feels over-long; but there is much to admire, not least the imaginative orchestration. It may be an exploratory work and, in some ways, lacking maturity, but the signs of the forthcoming greatness are there, and the piece now rightly takes its place in the orchestral repertoire with the other two concert-overtures of Elgar.

The Overture was completed in the July,[15] and the composer conducted the first performance at the Public Hall in Worcester on 9th September, 1890. In a Festival programme that contained many of the standard pieces, together with some inconsequential novelties, Elgar's work was included in the 'bits and pieces' secular programme, traditionally held on the Wednesday evening. The following paragraph from the *Annals of the Three Choirs* describes the event in detail:

> In the evening, when the only miscellaneous selection of music was given, Dr Parry's '*Ode to St Cecilia's Day*', written for the Leeds Festival shortly before, was

performed. The composer conducted, and the beauties of this admirable work were well displayed, the solos being finely sung by Miss Anna Williams and Mr Watkin Mills. The choir, later in the programme, gave a fine rendering of Dr C. Harford Lloyd's partsong, 'To Morning', for eight-part chorus unaccompanied, composed especially for this Festival. The solos included Beethoven's 'Ah Perfido', sung by Mrs Hutchinson; a scene from 'La Juive' by Mr Edward Lloyd; a duet from Gounod's 'Romeo and Juliette', for the two singers named; an Irish ditty and a German song by Mr Plunket Greene. The suite for orchestra, 'Peer Gynt', by Grieg, was well played, and the introduction to the third act of 'Lohengrin' carefully performed. A new overture, 'Froissart', composed and conducted by Mr E. Elgar, a Worcester musician, was included in the programme, and created a very favourable impression.[16]

It makes one feel exhausted just to read about it, but that was the way of the late Victorians - they enjoyed the variety of these marathon events. It would be interesting to know what was passing through their minds when their miscellaneous pleasures were to be interrupted by a serious composition from a 'local lad'. Elgar himself must surely have experienced both apprehension and enormous pride at that memorable moment that he rose from the violins to take the baton. The corner had indeed been turned.

On the whole the reviews were favourable, most of them suggesting that Elgar was a composer to watch for the future, with some reservations on the musical content. The feared Joseph Bennett of *The Daily Telegraph* opined that 'Mr Elgar has ideas and feeling as well as aspiration, and should be encouraged to persevere. He will one day 'arrive'.'

Elgar was pleased with the work's reception, stressing that it was at least enjoyed by the musicians present! There can be no better account of this auspicious occasion than that given by the young Ivor Atkins, then assistant to George Robertson Sinclair (1863-1917) at Hereford:

> Never before had I heard such a wonderful combination of a first-rate Chorus and Orchestra. I was naturally specially interested in Elgar, knowing that he was to produce a new Overture whose very title attracted me, for I had just been reading Froissart's 'Chronicles'. Sinclair pointed Elgar out to me. There he was, fiddling among the first violins, with his fine intellectual face, his heavy moustache, his dark hair, his nervous eyes, and his beautiful sensitive hands. The Wednesday evening came. I had no dress clothes with me, having come over from Hereford for the day, so I crept up the steps leading to the back of the Orchestra and peeped from behind those on the platform. The new Overture was placed at the end of the first half of the programme.
>
> The great moment came, and I watched Elgar's shy entry on to the platform. From that moment my eyes did not leave him, and I listened to the Overture, hearing it in the exciting way one hears music when among the players. I heard the surge of the strings, the chatter of the woodwind, the sudden bursts from the horns, the battle call of the trumpets, the awesome beat of the drums and the thrill of the cymbal clashes. I was conscious of all these and of the

hundred and one other sounds from an orchestra that stir
one's blood and send one's heart into one's mouth.

But there was something else I was conscious of - I knew
that Elgar was the man for me, I knew that I completely
understood his music, and that my heart and soul went with
it.[17]

And there began a deep and lasting friendship between the musicians
that was to be of inestimable benefit to both, as well as to the Three Choirs
Festival.

Shortly after the Worcester commission the Elgars returned to
Worcester, with the disappointed composer renewing the life of a local
peripatetic teacher. The mission for glory had failed - albeit temporarily.
To compound the worries the *Overture 'Froissart'* was not eagerly seized
upon by the British orchestras, and it was ten years before it was included
in a London programme. It was also some time before Elgar took on
another large canvas with success and, although it was not written for a
Festival, the new work did have its first hearing in Worcester - the cantata,
The Black Knight, written for the Worcester Festival Choral Society and
its conductor, Hugh Blair.[18] For the text he turned to Longfellow's
translation of a German ballad, where again he was attracted to a tale of
chivalry, although here there is a touch of pathos in the story, together
with a questioning conclusion, elements which were to become prominent
factors through his series of major choral works in the coming years.

Elgar had been working at *The Black Knight* project for a couple of
years in the hope of gaining a foothold into the cantata market of the
British choral movement. Turning his back on Biblical subject material,
which had so dominated the Festival programmes of the nineteenth

century, Elgar preferred to explore a favoured poet of the time for his text. In this respect he was perhaps influenced by his rival, Charles Villiers Stanford (1852-1924), who had achieved enormous success with his secular cantata, *The Revenge*, to words by Tennyson. Sketches of *The Black Knight*, which Elgar significantly called a Symphony for Chorus and Orchestra, came to the notice of Hugh Blair who urged the composer to complete the work with the words: 'If you will finish it, I will produce it at Worcester.' Although the Elgars' regular holiday in Bavaria intervened, the work was completed by the end of January, 1893, and Blair was true to his word. Reviews of the first performance were only lukewarm, although the Worcester public apparently enthused over what appeared to be a fine performance.

The Black Knight was certainly more challenging than most of the dross that was presented to choralists at that time. Elgar himself was aware of the problems in performance for, in a letter to A.J. Jaeger at Novello's, he wrote: 'It is too artistic for the ordinary conductor of choral societies - I find they are an inordinately ignorant lot of cheesemongering idiots. The chorus and orchestra go for my things, but the conductors always, or nearly always, find them too difficult - to conduct'. Many of these maligned conductors attended the first performance, finding the work an attractive proposition for their societies and, as a result, *The Black Knight* was scheduled for performance in a number of venues, including Birmingham, Hereford, Walsall and Wolverhampton - mostly conducted by the composer!

A particular enthusiast was Dr Charles Swinnerton Heap (1847-1900), the leading choral trainer and conductor in the Midlands, whose principal work centred on Birmingham, Stoke-on-Trent and Wolverhampton, and who founded the North Staffordshire Music

Festival in 1888. To Heap should go the accolade for encouraging Elgar to progress to a larger choral undertaking for, following the success of *The Black Knight* with his various choral groups, he persuaded the composer to write a full-length work for his enterprising and flourishing Festival. As a result the 1896 North Staffordshire Festival included the première of *King Olaf*, Elgar's most substantial work to that point in his career, by which time the conductor and composer had become close friends. Heap, who showed an amazing empathy for Elgar's music, was appointed chorus master to the Birmingham Festival in 1895, and it would have been his task to prepare the chorus for the première of *The Dream of Gerontius*, but his sudden death early in 1900 threw the preparations into disarray, resulting in the notorious failure of the chorus at the first performance. The North Staffordshire Festival also died with Heap, although Elgar remained a firm favourite with the Potteries' singers and audiences for the remainder of his life.[19]

Another close friendship that had developed was with Hugh Blair (1864-1932), the young assistant at the Cathedral, who had virtually taken charge of Worcester's music as a result of Dr Done's infirmity. Blair was given the responsibility of directing most of the 1893 Festival at Worcester. His programme contained the obligatory *Elijah, Hymn of Praise, The Last Judgement* and *Messiah*; adventurous 'new' works to the Three Choirs' audiences were Bach's *Mass in B minor* and the *German Requiem* by Brahms. Also included was Parry's oratorio *Job* which, after the enormous success of its première at Gloucester in the previous year,[20] had become the 'flavour of the month'. This work achieved the rare distinction at the time of being presented at three successive Festivals. There were two first performances: Parry's *Overture to an Unwritten Tragedy* and a *Te Deum* by Blair. But Elgar was overlooked by the

Festival committee, in spite of his mounting recognition with *The Black Knight*, several splendid partsongs and the *Serenade for Strings*.[21] Naturally he was extremely disenchanted with the whole set-up, but agreed to play First Violin in the orchestra 'for the sake of the fee, as I could get no recognition as a composer'.[22] In fact, the name of E.W. Elgar would never appear again in the list of the Festival 'Band'.

In spite of the rejection from his 'home' festival, Elgar was entering into a period of rich vein with his compositions, and much of this was due to the friendships with Heap and Blair. We have already noted the commission for the North Staffordshire Festival, and Elgar worked sporadically at his chosen subject, but he also produced several smaller works of distinction. There was the splendidly ceremonial *Sursum Corda* for the visit of the Duke of York to Worcester Cathedral in April, 1894, some charming songs, the distinctive partsongs for high voices, violins and piano, *The Snow* and *Fly, singing-bird, fly,* and the *Organ Sonata* of 1895, a work which has become a favourite at the Festivals in recent times, for its importance is now widely recognised in the development of the composer's skills of formal construction on a large canvas. The Sonata[23] was the result of Blair's encouragement and persistence, even though the first performance to a party of visiting American organists in July, 1895, proved to be something of a disaster, for the virtuoso work was too much of a challenge for Blair, who had only four days to prepare it, and without doubt needed a large dose of 'Dutch courage' to assist him. Elgar was loyal to Blair though, repaying some of his debt to the younger man by orchestrating his *Advent Cantata*, a well-designed work which was first heard at the Worcester Festival of 1896.

Blair had been appointed organist at the Cathedral in 1895 on the death of Dr Done but, sadly had become addicted to the bottle, and an unsympathetic Dean and Chapter dismissed him in 1897. Clearly he was a most talented *kappelmeister*, for there is enough evidence of his dynamic conducting and vision in programme planning, with Elgar feeling strongly enough about him to write to a friend[24] that 'Blair and I are going to pull things together here, and make the place more lively'.

The annual Bavarian holidays prompted Alice to write a set of poems based on their experiences of local dancing and singing, and all designed to suit her husband's musical ideas. Edward set to work with enthusiasm, completing the set of choral songs known as *From the Bavarian Highlands* in a short space of time during the early spring of 1895. These delightful songs show a lighter side to Elgar's character: they are full of sunshine and happiness. Originally for piano accompaniment, Elgar orchestrated the songs in time for a first performance by the Worcester Festival Choral Society on 21st April, 1896, the first of several events in a momentous year that was to change his life.

The commission from the North Staffordshire Music Festival for the October of 1896 has already been mentioned, but Elgar could never have predicted that he would be asked to write another major work for that same year. The new commission was to write a choral work for the Worcester Festival of 1896. Clearly the friendship with Blair had some bearing on the invitation, for he was now fully in charge of the programming for this, his only, Three Choirs Festival as official conductor, but, as is often the case today, it is possible that the matter was discussed and confirmed on the golf course. Elgar frequently played golf with the Revd. T. Littleton Wheeler, then the secretary of the Three Choirs Festival at Worcester, and on one of the rounds the matter of a choral commission was broached; the formal invitation from Blair requested that the work should not be yet another cantata, but a full-scale oratorio.

Realising that he could not raid the poetic lines of a Longfellow or a Tennyson for this commission Elgar turned for assistance to the Revd. Edward Capel Cure in preparing the libretto. Capel Cure (1860-1949), a son-in-law of the Fittons of Malvern, whose daughter Isobel was shortly to figure in the *Enigma Variations* (number six), was a fine 'cellist, who, at the time that he had been a curate at Holy Trinity Church in Worcester, had played chamber music with Elgar; he subsequently became vicar of Bradninch in Devon, and it was from here that he advised Elgar on the text of his new oratorio. Three possible subjects were suggested – The Healing of the Blind Man from St John's Gospel, The Magi, and Saint Barnabas – and Elgar went along with Capel Cure's preference for the St John text, which would be modified and embellished by the author. The libretto was completed at some speed and sent to Elgar at his Garmisch holiday home, where the composer set to work immediately, even before he had received the official letter of commission from the Festival committee. The suggested title was *Lux Christi*, which was later changed, after much deliberation, to *The Light of Life*, in order to avoid any suggestion of a Roman Catholic allegory.

The text of *The Light of Life* is centred upon the heroic figure of the blind man, who is healed by Jesus, but the mere fact of the miracle created loneliness and rejection by his own people, suspicious of his new religious experiences. In the final reckoning it is the blind man's mother who emerges as the strongest character in the plot, having pleaded for her son's healing, and then courageously facing up to the ensuing criticism. In this, his first attempt at the portrayal of Christ, Elgar paints a strong character, devoid of the sentimentality so favoured by the lesser Victorian composers. It is fascinating to discover that the plot of *King Olaf* has similar implications. The Nordic hero, in spite of being a Christian – and outcast for his faith – was in fact something of a tyrant and womaniser, who ultimately meets his death in battle. Here too the final word of reconciliation is left with a mother figure, who had found solace in her grieving by becoming a nun. The significant difference between the libretti is in the conclusion, whereas Olaf's mission was unproductive, the Blind Man could justifiably be seen as a figure of hope.

Working at the two pieces in parallel, it was inevitable that there should be some cross-fertilization in textural images as well as in musical expression, and a close study of the two works will reveal many interesting points of comparison. Both compositions prove to be training grounds for the great oratorios that were to follow, but have many significant features in themselves. Of course there is the influence of Wagner in the dramatic moments, especially in the recitative passages, and romantic opera seems to be a governing factor in the heroic arias; some biographers have even suggested a link with Verdi's *Requiem*,[25] a work much admired by Elgar, yet the choral writing stems very definitely from the 'English tradition', as exemplified in the final chorus of *The Light of Life* and, dare one suggest it, the 'Sullivan-style' waltz music of 'A little bird in the air' from *King Olaf*. The gem of the oratorio is undoubtedly, and perhaps not surprisingly, the orchestral introduction, entitled *Meditation;* this is Elgar at his very best, and the intrusion of the male chorus into the final bars is a stroke of genius, reminiscent of the first choral entry in *The Dream of Gerontius. King Olaf* is no less original in its conception with the chorus in effect providing book-ends to the whole work, and the unexpected unaccompanied 'partsong' *As torrents in summer* preceding the final peroration is a magical touch.

Elgar worked at both works side by side, with *King Olaf* being the first to achieve completion, but the vocal score of *The Light of Life* was ready for the publishers in early April, and the composer began work on the full score[26] in early May. At about that time the composer was visited by the well-known Birmingham journalist, Robert Buckley, who noted that:

> The Worcester Festival was due in a few months, and the composer felt that much depended on this, his first choral work to be heard at an important meeting. . . . *King Olaf* was in hand, and the tent[27] was littered with sheets of music-paper bearing myriad pencil marks, undecipherable to the stranger as the hieroglyphics on a blackbird's egg, and, like the proverbial lost pocket-book, of no use to any one but the owner. Of a fugue in *The Light of Life* he said: 'I thought a fugue would be expected of me. The British public would hardly tolerate oratorio without a fugue. So I tried to give them one. Not a 'barn-door' fugue, but one with an independent accompaniment. There's a bit of a canon, too, and in short, I hope there's enough counterpoint to give the real British respectability![28]

Edward appeared to be well pleased with his new oratorio, and was aware of its importance at this crucial time in his career: it was almost his 'last chance'. He did the rounds of choral rehearsals at Gloucester, Hereford and Worcester, as well as travelling to Leeds a fortnight before the Festival to work with the northern contingent, who were still retained by the Worcester committee. This fragmentation of the chorus may have been unsatisfactory, but at least Elgar made some useful contacts while in the North – contacts that would ultimately lead to his involvement with the flourishing Triennial Musical Festival at Leeds.

The inadequate time spent together by the singers made for a very insecure chorus, and this particular festival was considered to be one of the worst in terms of choral preparation, even though *The Light of Life* seemed to escape the worst of the inefficiencies. At least Elgar was allocated some of the finest soloists of the time – Anna Williams (the mother); Jessie King (narrator); Edward Lloyd (the blind man), and Watkin Mills (Jesus); they had joined the orchestra for the London rehearsal, which had been attended by several prominent musicians. Word got out that the new work was something rather special, the *Worcester Daily Times*[29] reporting that 'Mr Edward Lloyd says it is one of the finest English works composed for some time, and that the instrumentation is particularly fine. The tenor part is the finest he has had presented to him for many years. Signor Randegger,[30] after hearing the first rehearsal in London, said he thought it was the best English work that had been produced within his knowledge for certainly twenty years.'

The eagerly awaited first performance took place on Tuesday, 8th September, 1896, conducted by the composer; it was the first piece in a programme that also contained selections from Handel's *Samson*. Sadly, the attendance was very disappointing; the musical public obviously had as little stomach then for a new work as it does at the end of the millennium! But the critics were in attendance, and some interesting comments were made, most of the criticism being reserved for the text, which, like the libretti in most of Elgar's early choral works, was admittedly fairly elementary, if not banal. One critic, the Precentor of Worcester Cathedral,[31] even suggested that certain passages were 'absolutely irreverent'. The reviews of the music were more encouraging. The *Musical Times*[32] stated:

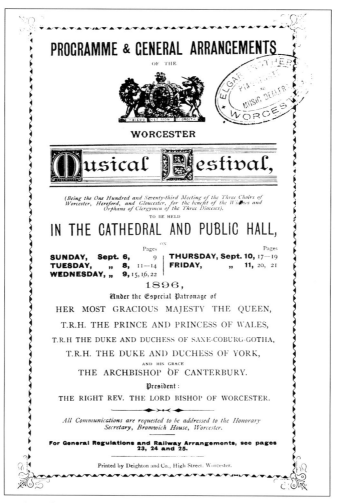

The title page of the Worcester 1896 Festival Programme
– bearing the stamp of the Elgar Brothers' High Street shop

TUESDAY EVENING, SEPTEMBER 8th, at 7.30 o'clock.

IN THE CATHEDRAL.

PART I.

THE LIGHT OF LIFE (Lux Christi),
Edward Elgar.

A SHORT ORATORIO,

Composed for this Festival.

Founded on the ninth chapter of S. John.   The Libretto arranged by the REV.
E. CAPEL-CURE, M.A.

Conducted by the Composer.

THE BLIND MAN (Tenor) - - - - - - -	Mr. EDWARD LLOYD
THE CHRIST (Baritone)- - - - - - - -	Mr. WATKIN MILLS
THE MOTHER OF THE BLIND MAN (Soprano) -	Miss ANNA WILLIAMS
NARRATOR (Contralto) - - - - - - - -	Miss JESSIE KING

MEDITATION—ORCHESTRA	
CHORUS (Levites within the Temple)................	{ Seek Him that maketh the seven stars
SOLO—Mr. EDWARD LLOYD	O Thou, in heaven's dome
RECITATIVE—Miss JESSIE KING	As Jesus passed by
CHORUS (Disciples)	Who did sin ?
SOLO—Miss ANNA WILLIAMS	Be not extreme
SOLO—Mr. WATKIN MILLS	Neither hath this man sinned
CHORUS	Light out of darkness
RECITATIVE—Miss JESSIE KING and Mr. WATKIN MILLS	} And when He had thus spoken
CHORUS (Soprani and Contralti).......................	Doubt not thy Father's care
SCENE—Miss JESSIE KING, Mr. EDWARD LLOYD and CHORUS	} He went his way therefore
SOLO—Mr. EDWARD LLOYD	As a spirit didst Thou pass
RECITATIVE—Miss JESSIE KING	They brought him to the Pharisees
CHORUS	This man is not of God
SOLO—Miss JESSIE KING	Thou only hast the words of life
SCENE—Miss ANNA WILLIAMS, Miss JESSIE KING, Mr. EDWARD LLOYD and CHORUS	} But the Jews did not believe
SOLO—Miss ANNA WILLIAMS, and CHORUS OF WOMEN	} Woe to the shepherds of the flock
RECITATIVE—Miss JESSIE KING, Mr. EDWARD LLOYD and Mr. WATKIN MILLS	} Jesus heard that they had cast him out
SOLO—Mr. WATKIN MILLS.....	I am the Good Shepherd
CHORUS	Light of the World

*The programme page for the first performance of
'The Light of Life' – Worcester 1896*

Does not the composer live near Worcester, and has he not yet to make a famous name? Facts of this kind were against him, but Mr Elgar, I hope, understands how 'to labour and to wait.' Time is on his side, and my trust is that, as years pass, he will make the best use of increasing experience in all that concerns the character and method of his art. . . . He is not a wayside musician whom we can afford to pass and forget, but one to be watched, encouraged, and, as he is still a young man, counselled. . . . Mr Elgar is not yet a master of oratorio, and the reason is partly to be discovered, perhaps, in the fact indicated by his new work, that his sympathies are much more with the orchestration than with voices.

The Sunday Times[33] perhaps echoed more the feelings of those who were in attendance on that memorable day:

Seldom does one dip into the 'local art' lottery to yield a prize so conspicuously promising as Mr Edward Elgar. Here is a musician of whom Worcester has perfect reason to be proud, and the place accorded to his short oratorio *The Light of Life* in Tuesday evening's programme was eminently justified by the critical verdict of the following day. The young Malvern music teacher has uncommon talent. He knows his Wagner well – sometimes, perhaps, a trifle too well, and he has turned his experience as an orchestral player to good account; hence the marked superiority of his scoring as compared with his vocal

writing . . . but his sense of proportion and tone colour, and
his knowledge of effect are quite exceptional . . . this is of
such excellence that I cannot help looking to Mr Elgar for a
really fine work when he comes across a 'book' which
appeals in every sense to his strong artistic temperament.

That book was to be *The Dream of Gerontius*, now less than four
years away. However, neither it, nor any other major work would be
written for a Three Choirs Festival. Elgar's early experiences of the
Festival at Worcester had created the opportunity and foundation on
which he could build his musical personality and distinctive style,
particularly with regard to learning orchestral techniques and sonorities;
but whether he appreciated this fact is open to some doubt.

The first performance of *King Olaf* followed eight weeks later,
attaining an even greater degree of acceptance from both audiences and
critics, the greatest accolade coming from the pen of Joseph Bennett in
The Daily Telegraph:[34]

Behind all his work lies the power of living talent, the
charm of individuality in art, and the pathos of one who, in
utter simplicity, pours forth that which he feels constrained
to say.... Almost every number was applauded fervently....

It is extraordinary that these two works gradually fell into oblivion,
(not a note of *King Olaf* has ever been heard at a Three Choirs Festival),
being overshadowed by the more celebrated masterpieces that emerged
over the following twelve years or so, but it was good to experience the
surprise and delight of the audiences at the quality of these pieces in their

centenary performances[35] during 1996. As Michael Kennedy has written :[36]

> *The Light of Life* has not received the attention from Elgar
> commentators which is its due. The concentration has been
> on its defects and immaturities rather than on its strengths
> and virtues.

The same could be said of *King Olaf* which, if anything, was nearer to the conception of *The Dream of Gerontius*, now very firmly in Elgar's creative mind. 1896 was a remarkable year for Elgar; would he be able to build upon these successes? The spirit was there, the ambition was there, the talent was there; on the strength of these fine works, the public was surely now ready to accept that there was a genius in their midst. And surely the Three Choirs Festival committees would now realise that Elgar had the potential to be their icon for the new century which was fast approaching? They needed him as much as he had needed them.

3

The Vintage Years

'I fear I can do nothing . . . you see I am too near Worcester to be in it . . . I'm a steward and subscribe . . . but you may rely on me to do my best to introduce sterling stuff . . . Anything 'genuine' and natural pleases me . . . the stuff I hate and which I know is ruining any chance for good music in England is like Stanford's, which is neither fish, flesh, fowl, nor good red herring.'[37]

From 1896 Elgar was ever-present at the Three Choirs Festival, as composer/conductor, or member of the audience. He was always a steward at Worcester, but he clearly felt that he could wield little influence over the policy making and programme planning of a committee who were very protective of their power and rights. The above extract indicates that he had something of a love/hate relationship with his fellow stewards on what he perceived to be an entrenched attitude with regard to their lack of vision; the jibe at Stanford was really a general remark against the academic composers, who tended to hold centre stage at most of the British Festivals with their prolific note-spinning, and who Elgar felt were stifling the opportunities of more talented composers. In another letter to Jaeger he claimed that a work by the American composer, Horatio Parker,[38] contained 'more *music* than any of your other Englishmen have as yet managed to knock out, including Parry, Stanford and MacKenzie – these great men seem to be busily employed in performing one another's works – no one else will.' [39]

Any regrets that Elgar might have harboured on the sudden departure of Hugh Blair would have been allayed by the appointment of the 27 year-old Ivor Atkins (1869-1953)[40], already a friend and admirer. It might be a matter for conjecture whether Elgar had had a hand in his preferment, although there is little evidence to suggest that he had any great influence over the machinations of the Worcester Dean and Chapter. He was certainly responsible for a similar Hereford appointment some years later.

With Sinclair in his early thirties at Hereford, and the recently-appointed Herbert Brewer (1865-1928)[41] of a similar age at Gloucester, Elgar found himself involved with a trio of young enthusiasts, who were to guide the Festival into a new century with a new image, for which he would find himself the principal protagonist. During the period up to the First World War, and following his successes of 1896, Elgar had suddenly become the dominant celebrity of the Festivals, a role with which he would be identified until his death, in spite of his frequent rumblings of discontent with the system. Although no one could have predicted it at the beginning of 1897, Elgar had already written his major works for the Festival - only a handful of pieces were to receive first performances in the future, and none were actual commissions; he was either too pre-occupied writing other major works, or took the tactful line of declining, for it clearly rankled him that Three Choirs 'commissions' were deemed to be for the privilege, and not for any financial reward. However,

Sinclair did manage to procure a promise from Elgar of a pair of works for the Opening Service at Hereford in 1897, the first time that any of his music had been given at a Festival away from his home town; the *Te Deum* and *Benedictus* were the outcome of this request.

This was the year of Queen Victoria's Golden Jubilee, and Elgar was already committed to the writing of some celebratory works for his publisher, Novellos; these were the cantata *The Banner of Saint George* and an *Imperial March*. The first, to a text by the Bristol poet, Shapcott Wensley, was meant to provide a work that could be performed by all sorts and conditions of choral groups throughout the year of revelry. Elgar had never worked to order before, but he did fulfil the terms of the commission, even if the result proved to be something of a disappointment in his output, not least because of the jingoistic nature of the text, which certainly fits uncomfortably into present-day thinking. The March was a different matter, although in some ways – as the title suggests – it expresses an even more expressive patriotism; but it drew out the best of Elgar in orchestration and nobility of utterance, and certainly proved to be the starting point for the *Pomp and Circumstance* marches which were to follow shortly. Again it was intended that the *Imperial March* should be a focal point for orchestral concerts during the year, but it is interesting that it was not heard outside London until the Opening Service of the Hereford Festival on 12th September, some five months after its first performance at the Crystal Palace.

The *Te Deum* and *Benedictus* appeared at that same Service, all conducted by the composer. With his other obligations it is not surprising that Elgar did not begin work on the canticles immediately after receiving the invitation from Sinclair, and it was not until early June that he took the pieces to Sinclair for approval. Percy Hull (1878-1968)[42], then

Sinclair's pupil, was present on the occasion of Elgar's visit, recalling it in the following words:

> I was privileged to hear Elgar play over his *Festival Te Deum* and *Benedictus* in Sinclair's house to see whether the work would be acceptable for the programme of the Festival at Hereford. He was as nervous as a kitten and heaved a huge sigh of relief when Sinclair said: 'It is *very, very* modern, but I think it will do; you shall play it again after supper when Hull and I will give you our final verdict.' All this in Sinclair's, stammering and somewhat patronising fashion.[43]

The disparaging remarks on the modernity of the settings seem rather extreme, for Elgar had modelled the works on the expectation of the Anglican tradition, with a hint of his previous choir and organ experiences at St George's Roman Catholic Church in Worcester. Both canticles are conceived on a large scale and, as could be predicted, the orchestration is subtle and imaginative, perhaps helping to disguise the fact that some of the choral writing is predictable by Elgar's own high standards. The knowledgeable listener will be able to point to influences from S.S. Wesley and Hubert Parry (the lengthy introduction and first choral entry to the *Te Deum* bears some resemblance to *Blest Pair of Sirens*) and, dare one mention it, C.V. Stanford. But there are also some Elgarian innovative touches, not least the thematic relationship between the canticles, and the inspirational transference of the gentle ending of the *Te Deum* to the opening material of the *Benedictus;* indeed, there were several significant improvements of style and method over the Worcester oratorio of the previous year. In any event, Novellos were prepared to publish the canticles in time for the Festival, and it was the ensuing correspondence that cemented the friendship between Elgar and Jaeger[44]. On receipt of the full score the latter had written effusively to Elgar, later expressing his disappointment at the fee offered by his firm, eliciting the following reply:

> Please do not feel that I am a disappointed person, either commercially or artistically - what I feel is the utter want of *sympathy* - they, i.e. principally critics, lump me with people I abhor - mechanics. Now my music, such as it is, is alive, you say it has heart - I always say to my wife (over any piece or passage of my work that pleases me) 'if you cut that it would bleed!' *You* seem to see that, but who else does?[45]

Jaeger was so taken with the canticles that he made the long journey from Huddersfield to Hereford to attend the first performance. His reactions were expressed in this extract from his congratulatory letter:

> I hunted for you high and low during the Service (awfully long!) and afterwards, but you were not to be seen. Never mind, I spent a most delightful 22 hours in the delightful cathedral town and I have heard your finest, most spontaneous and most deeply felt and most effective work, and I was *very happy*.[46]

There began a close friendship, much of it conducted in

correspondence, giving a graphic picture of musical life at the turn of that century, some important glimpses of the Three Choirs' atmosphere and intrigues, as well as giving telling portraits of the composer and his publisher. Elgar desperately needed Jaeger's powers of persuasion and perceptive comments for, although his career had now taken wing, he still remained full of uncertainties and reservations.

The public response to the new works was no more than a placid acceptance, and the fact that they appeared as part of the ceremonial and social opening to the Festival would have created little more than a passing interest (or even intrusion) into the minds of many in attendance. The critics gave the pieces a mixed reception, the *Morning Post* summing up what most of them felt by suggesting that they sounded more like 'a warlike song of triumph than an expression of Christian praise and prayer' - an unjust reaction, showing a complete misunderstanding of the composer's intentions, or the occasion for which the works were designed. It is true that the canticles have not enjoyed the popularity of many of the other shorter choral works of Elgar, but much of this is due to the fact that, although they sound well with organ accompaniment, they are too long and elaborate for normal liturgical use; but they do make fine recital pieces, and could well provide a satisfying 'filler' in a choral concert. They have appeared from time to time at the Festival Opening Services, usually – and appropriately – at Hereford.

One of the visitors to the 1897 Festival was Nicholas Kilburn[47], who was to become a close and influential friend to Elgar. Another was the cathedral robin, described by Elgar as one of the 'festival musicians'; after inventing an extra part for Schubert's *Unfinished Symphony*, the robin was caught and caged, the intention being to free him at the end of the week. Sadly, in Elgar's words 'he pined away, and died.'

Brewer's first festival at Gloucester in 1898 was fairly ambitious, in spite of the financial restrictions imposed upon him by the Stewards, but Elgar did not figure in his original plans. A group of composers had been invited to offer works for the festival and when one of them, Rosalind Ellicott (1857-1924)[48], dropped out, Brewer invited Elgar to provide a short orchestral work. The response was terse and immediate:

Forli

Malvern

17 April, 1898

Dear Mr Brewer,

I have received a request from the Secretary to write a short orchestral work for the Evening Concert. I am sorry I am too busy to do so.

I wish, wish, wish, you would ask Coleridge-Taylor to do it. He still wants recognition and is far away the cleverest fellow amongst the young men. Please don't let your Committee throw away the chance of doing a good act!

Yours sincerely,

Edward Elgar[49]

Brewer hesitated for some time, and the eventual invitation to Samuel Coleridge-Taylor (1875-1912)[50] presented the young composer with the daunting and unreasonable task of preparing his most important composition to date in just three months. In spite of this he produced the *Ballade in A minor* for orchestra, which was enthusiastically received, giving him the start that he needed in his tragically short career. He was the first of many composers who were to benefit from Elgar's recommendation to the festival committees.

The Elgars attended most of the concerts, but Edward's only contribution was to conduct the Meditation from *The Light of Life* at the Opening Service, albeit the first time that any of his music had been heard at Gloucester. Yet another friendship was to develop from this festival for the Elgars stayed at Hasfield Court with William Meath Baker (1858-1935), a previous acquaintance and near neighbour of Alice's Gloucestershire family. His generous hospitality was recognised by Elgar in 'W.M.B' – number four of the *Enigma Variations*, soon to be conceived.

Elgar's refusal to write for this Festival was almost certainly due to the fact that he was immersed in his new commission for the famous Leeds Festival, due to take place in the October of 1898. The Festival had begun in 1858, coinciding with the opening of the imposing Town Hall by Queen Victoria; the grand concert hall was the pride of Yorkshire. Mainly choral in content the Festival continued triennially until 1953 (with the exception of the war years), and was revived and revitalised in 1958 by the Earl of Harewood. The nineteenth century witnessed commissions from Dvořák, Massenet, Parry, Stanford and Sullivan, among others, and some of this country's great choral masterpieces, such as Vaughan Williams' *Sea Symphony* (1910), Holst's *Choral Symphony* (1925), and Walton's *Belshazzar's Feast* (1931), were inspired by the Festival in the twentieth century. The renowned Yorkshire choral tradition also produced some spectacular singing, so it was inevitable that these skills should be sought elsewhere, and, as we have already noted, Leeds singers made a notable contribution to the Three Choirs Festival through the latter half of the century, although in doing so probably thwarted the ambitions of local talent.

There can be little doubt that the Leeds commission was considered by the composer to be the greatest challenge that he had so far encountered, even though he would have preferred to write a piece for orchestra rather than the choral work which was demanded. The Leeds Triennial Musical Festival was held in the highest esteem throughout the musical world, and most composers coveted a commission from it: Elgar was no exception, even though the success of his earlier cantatas with Yorkshire choirs had more or less ensured his ultimate recognition by this illustrious body. Choral commitment and careful preparation were assured, the publicity surrounding the event was second to none, and the Festival, in Sir Arthur Sullivan,[51] had the distinction of having one of the most revered musicians in England as its principal conductor. It was an ideal platform for the composer, now in his forties, to prove himself, and he availed himself of the opportunity, although at the cost of his health and temper.

Elgar agonised over the subject matter, considering both 'The Flight into Egypt' and 'Saint Augustine', but eventually decided on the story of the first century British leader Caractacus, who was ultimately defeated by the invaders and taken in captivity to Rome. The theme afforded a further opportunity of continuing the mood of patriotism generated by the recent Jubilee, and it also meant that he was able to infuse the music with his deep affection for the Malvern Hills, where much of the story's action takes place. He turned to Harry Arbuthnot Acworth[52] to assist him in compiling the text, the result proving wholly satisfying, even if some of the language is quaint to our modern ears. Suggesting that the humiliation of defeat in the final scene should be seen as a great victory was rather extravagant, but Elgar insisted that the work should end on a patriotic note - and he knew only too well how to express those sentiments in music. There is so much fine music in a work which is clearly operatically influenced (indeed, Elgar did consider adapting it for the stage), but the two scenes that stand out are the composer's own favourite *Woodland Scene* – the movement that captures his Worcestershire countryside better than any other that he wrote– and the *Triumphal March*, which surely rivals Verdi's march from Act Two of *Aida* for generating ceremonial fervour.

Following the first performance[53], conducted by the composer, critical comments were generally enthusiastic, even if the composer seemed remarkably subdued afterwards. The *Leeds Mercury* reported that

> It was a triumph, and everybody admitted it. Exclamations were to be heard all over the crowded hall and after the conclusion of every scene . . . hands were clapped as seldom they are in evening-dress circles, and the chorus rose en masse and cheered Mr Elgar for all he was worth. The composer was most modest. His bow was hurried, almost nervous, and he seemed only too glad to be able to get away from it all.[54]

At least he had the satisfaction of knowing that a London performance was promised even before the work had been played in Leeds - a rare bonus for the doubting composer. It was Elgar's last and greatest cantata, and it was wholly appropriate that the Queen should graciously accept its dedication. The composer was now deservedly recognised in court circles, and he stood on the threshold of a glorious time in his career.

Caractacus was not a work which would be likely to feature in a Three Choirs programme[55] at those times; indeed it was nearly another eighty years before it graced a festival programme – and that at a Gloucester leisure centre during a thunderstorm! Twelve years later it appeared again at Gloucester, but this time in the Cathedral, without objection; after all, is it so sinful or disrespectful to the Almighty to be patriotic?

As a result of the success of this major work, together with Elgar's new-found standing in the community, the question must have arisen whether he had grown away from his provincial roots, and whether the Three Choirs would ever again be able to hold his attentions. In fact any fears that were held were dispersed by the rumours circulating that Elgar was writing a symphony for the Worcester Festival of 1899.

Frustrated at his failure to attract a commission for an orchestral work, Elgar had written to Atkins offering a symphony for the next festival at Worcester: the theme of the work was to be General Charles Gordon. A man of stern religious faith, who spoke out strongly against slavery, a benefactor of the poor, and possessed with great military prowess, Gordon was the sort of heroic figure likely to appeal to Elgar's sensibilities, and there was added interest in the known fact that the General had read Cardinal Newman's poem *The Dream of Gerontius* shortly before his death in the massacre at Khartoum in 1885. Elgar began preliminary sketches on the symphony, but his heart was not really in the project, and he was still complaining to Jaeger and others that his work was under-valued and that he was 'hard up'. In any event a commission had arrived from Randegger to write a work for the 1899 Norwich Festival, and an enquiry had been received from the celebrated

Birmingham Festival for a major work in 1900, probably the greatest accolade that a composer could receive at that time in the field of choral music. So he had more than enough incentive to exercise his artistic powers - and be paid for doing so! But he had also become absorbed in a personal project which had come about more or less by accident – the *Variations on an Original Theme* (later to be subtitled *Enigma*). This was something that he could write for himself – there were no pressures of deadlines, or strings attached to local demands and conditions. He worked at this new venture with enormous enthusiasm and vigour from the first jottings in October of 1898 to the finished orchestration in the middle of February the following year. He was well-pleased with the finished product.

The story of the *Enigma Variations* - a unique portrayal of friends in music – is too familiar to warrant elaboration here, but its story is finalised at the 1899 Worcester Festival. Following the first sensational performance in London under Richter, it became apparent to Jaeger that the final variation was inconclusive and too short. Appeals to the composer to rethink this variant were stubbornly refused at first, but gradually Elgar accepted the argument of his editor. The importance of Jaeger's advising, admonishing, inspiring and urging was one of the prime factors in Elgar's rising stardom, and he was right again in this instance. The last movement was extended, and the first performance of the *Enigma Variations* as we know it today was premièred in the Public Hall at Worcester on 13 September, conducted by the composer for the first time.[56] To programme this masterpiece in his first festival programme was a great feather in the cap of Ivor Atkins who, having swallowed his disappointment at the non-arrival of the symphony, saw the potential of the *Variations* when he heard the London performance.

The 'Gordon' Symphony had been withdrawn from the proposed programme as late as May, the minute of the committee meeting reading:

> The Conductor reported that Mr Elgar found it impossible to carry out his promise to write a new Symphony, and the sub-committee decided instead to include in the programme Mr Elgar's Light of Life . . . [57]

The oratorio was also to undergo some alterations. Following the textual criticisms of the first performance three years previously, there were substantial changes to the libretto which necessitated some rewriting of the vocal lines. Again it is this version which now constitutes the standard publication. So the Worcester Festival was responsible for putting the finishing touches to two of Elgar's principal works. The Wednesday of the Festival transpired to be the 'Elgar day', for the oratorio was given during the morning concert, and the *Variations* appeared as the centre-piece of the evening's secular concert. But it was the latter that grabbed the listening public's imagination. Mrs Richard Powell ('Dorabella' – number nine of the *Enigma*) paints a charming picture of the event in the following quotation from her book:[58]

> That September it was Worcester's turn for the Three Choirs Festival, and the Variations were down for the Wednesday Concert in the Public Hall. . . . There were several of 'us' there and my stepmother came down for it too. As she had three relations - brother, brother-in-law, and step-daughter – 'Variants', and at least three friends besides, it is no wonder she wished to be present. I sat with W.M.B

and I am afraid we did not behave very well; it was not easy to do so sitting next to him as he always saw the funny side of everything. He was immensely interested and amused by 'R.B.T'., obviously seeing the likeness but quite at a loss - as we all were at first - to know how the likeness had been contrived. . . .

He did not understand his own variation, that was clear, nor did the rest of the party. I shall never forget the gauntlet that I had to run afterwards, at the Star Hotel, Worcester, where we were all staying for the Concert. He wanted to know what each variation meant including his own, and I was put in a very awkward position, with my father and stepmother (W.M.B's sister) there as I could not possibly have told them what I knew about them, they would not have understood. . . I cannot remember how many other 'Variations' I saw that evening, but I think it was a pretty fair gathering of the clan. It was a splendid performance, and E.E was right, he *had* orchestrated us well, and No. X was so lovely that I felt - that first time - that I wanted to hide somewhere. . . Of all Elgar's music the *Variations* bring back most vividly the memories of those enchanting days and the honour that was mine to be one of that company of fourteen friends.

As already mentioned earlier in this chapter Elgar's influence on this particular Festival was also extended to the programming of Horatio Parker's *Hora Novissima*, conducted by the composer, the first American to be accorded recognition at this historic Festival. It was an astute move on Elgar's part, for it brought American interest in the Festival which has never wavered since, and it brought to British attention a fine composer, whose subsequent neglect is hard to comprehend.[59] The title of the work may also have had some significance in Elgar's mind as he contemplated his own future masterwork.

Other Elgar influences in this programme cannot really be ascertained, but a further appearance of Coleridge-Taylor with his *Prelude for Orchestra* must have been a spin-off from the previous year's success at Gloucester. Elgar could hardly gain credit for the inclusion of *Elijah* and *Messiah*, as much as he admired them, for they remained obligatory. They were as essential to the success of the Festival (and the demands of the conservative Stewards) then as the work which now occupied Elgar's thoughts would be to the coming century of festivals.

With the Birmingham commission now assuming an air of urgency, Elgar was undecided if he should elaborate on his sketches for Cardinal Newman's poem, which had been exercising his mind for several years, or concentrate on designing the first part of his projected trilogy of New Testament oratorios. Both possibilities were put to the Birmingham committee, who apparently rather favoured the latter scheme, probably still disappointed that Dvořák had turned down their request to set *The Dream of Gerontius* for their 1888 Festival.[60] The problem now facing Elgar was one of libretto for *The Apostles*, a subject which had fascinated him since his childhood, especially the character of Judas. He turned once again to Capel Cure, but it soon became clear that the priest was unenthusiastic about the project, not least because of the limited time available to prepare such a massive undertaking. All this caused Elgar to retreat into one of his predictably negative moods, even to the point of resigning from the commission. However, Birmingham were not to be denied, subsequent negotiations persuading the reluctant composer to proceed with *The Dream of Gerontius* scheme. The financial arrangements were agreed, the publishing rights were negotiated to the composer's satisfaction, and he was assured that the Roman Catholic subject matter would present no problems. It remained to consult Fr. Neville, the executor for Cardinal Newman, for permission to condense the text of the 900-line verse, making it practical to set to music, but without losing the essential message of the poem. Elgar's suggestions were accepted and he began working in earnest early in the new year.

Although writing with intense concentration and remarkable speed, Elgar still found time to attend or conduct concerts of his own music. Following the triumph of the *Enigma Variations*, he had achieved another enormous success with his Norwich commission of the previous October. Randegger had changed the assignment, seeking a work involving his 'star' soloist, Clara Butt (1872-1936), rather than the production of yet another cantata; Elgar readily accepted the change, writing *The Sea Pictures* for the redoubtable soloist. For all their outward attraction, the songs were nevertheless charged with nostalgia, pathos, and wonder - a sort of reaction to the largely extrovert *Variations*. However, the songs, which are really Elgar's equivalent of Mahler's *Leider eines fahrenden Gesellen*[61], were immediately programmed by several singers and orchestras, and have remained firmly in the repertoire ever since, although surprisingly neglected in Three Choirs Festival planning.[62]

With such a gigantic undertaking on his drawing board it is not surprising that Elgar's participation in the 1900 Hereford Festival was rather limited. He conducted scene 3 from *Caractacus* at the secular concert, and his *Te Deum* and *Benedictus* were sung again at the Opening Service. There is no evidence that Sinclair had asked Elgar for any 'novelties' on this occasion, nor a suggestion of including any more of his music in a programme that had a patriotic theme in celebration of the 'noble achievements of the British Forces in South Africa'; had Elgar not been pre-occupied with greater things he would surely have been an ideal choice to contribute music for such a national mood of rejoicing. So the Stewards turned to Parry and Stanford, but there were significant works from Elgar's protégés Horatorio Parker and Coleridge-Taylor, and a performance of Verdi *Requiem* which was so impressive that it moved distinguished personages in the audience, including Elgar, to send a message of affectionate greetings to the composer.

The Elgars attended much of the Festival, but clearly the composer's attentions were centred on the forthcoming première of *The Dream of Gerontius* at Birmingham a few weeks later; indeed, he interrupted his stay at Hereford to take a chorus rehearsal in Birmingham The story of the disastrous first performance of Elgar's masterpiece is familiar enough, but fortunately there were enough discerning musicians and critics in attendance to recognise the work's worth, one of the most interesting comments being contributed by the German critic, Otto Lessman, who wrote:

> If I mistake not, the coming man has already arisen in the English musical world, an artist who has instinctively freed himself from the scholasticism which, till now, has held English art firmly bound in its fetters, an artist who has thrown open mind and heart to the great achievements which the mighty tone-masters of the century now departed have left us as a heritage for the one to come - Edward Elgar, the composer of The Dream of Gerontius.[63]

A new style of oratorio had been born, and a 'Three Choirs man' had created it, although he could scarcely have imagined how revered this Catholic work would become in those exalted circles which had bred him, yet who had even objected to a Latin title for his first festival oratorio. But, as we shall discover, a few hurdles still had to be negotiated before *The Dream of Gerontius* would be universally accepted into the festival repertoire.

Brewer might have considered the oratorio for 1901, but fell back on the 'safe' suggestion of including the *Prelude* and *Angel's Farewell* at the Opening Service. He eventually invited Elgar to conduct his new overture *Cockaigne*[64] at the secular concert, a work which had been written in the aftermath of the *Gerontius* disappointments, and at a time when he was renewing his distrust of the local societies. An extract from a letter to Jaeger paints a depressing picture of music-making in his local environment:

> . . . I am bored to death with commonplace ass-music down here - the bucolics are all right when they don't attempt more than eat, drink and sleep, but beyond these things they fail . . . [65]

A strange reaction to the people who had really supported him though all his trials and tribulations and now rejoiced in his success, but there must have been some deep-rooted reason for his offence. *Cockaigne* had given him a chance to 'cock a snook' at these people, and presumably their provincial festivities as well, for it dwelt on the vigorous healthy life of the capital city, and provided an opportunity to offer some gratitude to the 'real' musicians, for the work is inscribed 'To my friends the members of British orchestras.' When played at Gloucester it was apparently the highlight of the concert.

Elgar's own music might have featured lightly in that Festival, but he did make a magnanimous gesture, as was his wont, to the festival conductor, whose cantata *Emmaus* had been commissioned by the Stewards.

There had been copyright difficulties over the libretto, which had been compiled by Joseph Bennett (1831-1911)[66]; when the problems had been resolved, time was getting short. The work was completed but, due to his heavy commitments with the Festival and a period of illness, Brewer had not scored a note of the cantata. Faced with withdrawing the work from the programme, Brewer received a note from Elgar offering to complete the orchestration, saying 'I know it's a cheek to offer, but if I can save you a little worry let me do so.' Not surprisingly Brewer readily accepted this 'generous act'. In early July, in less than a month, Elgar completed the scoring: in the covering letter to Brewer he wrote:

> I have taken great pleasure in trying to interpret your thoughts and feelings and only hope I have not grossly misrepresented them. Now: please accept my work on your score and never think I want any return whatever: keep a kind thought for a fellow sometime - that's all.[67]

The copyright problems continued almost up to the time of the first performance, but *Emmaus* was given on the Thursday of the Festival with a star-studded cast of soloists, receiving much acclaim. The work was repeated at Gloucester in 1907 with similar success. After Brewer's death the score and parts were lost, but were eventually found in the archive department of the Gloucester City Library by Anthony Boden when he was researching for his recent history of the Festival. As a result of this discovery *Emmaus* was revived at the Gloucester Festival in 1992[68]. Time had not dealt too kindly with much of the musical content, for the solo and choral writing appeared rather tame and too much imbued with a legacy of the nineteenth century cantata market, but Elgar's hand is unmistakeable, rescuing the work from being of mere curiosity value.

The Elgars attended most of the concerts at that Gloucester Festival although, never really comfortable in the body of the audience, they had found a spot in the Triforium where they could listen without distraction. At Hereford and Worcester the composer would always be able to seek solace behind the stage, his favourite spot at Worcester being commemorated by the site of his memorial window. Edward and Alice again stayed at Hasfield Court with the Baker family. By all accounts a most entertaining week was heightened by the unusually relaxed composer, who helped to enact historical plays in the gardens with the members of the house party. It was also the first festival at which the composer appeared as Dr Elgar, having received the honorary degree from Cambridge University the previous November. In spite of the supposed rivalry, even hostility, between Elgar and Stanford, it was the latter, in his capacity as Professor of Music at Cambridge, who had recommended the honour, even though he absented himself from the ceremony. The reasons for the much-documented disagreements between the two composers have never been convincingly established, other than resentment at Stanford's famous remark that *Gerontius* 'stinks of incense'; perhaps Elgar also saw in him the epitome of all that he considered to be false about musical academics. They certainly shared admiration for some of each other's music. The fact that Elgar's own doctorate might prove to be something of an impediment to his free thinking was a cause of some concern to him when it was first offered, but the fact that he picked up a host of doctorates and other academic awards throughout the remainder of his life suggested that he learnt to live with the problem!

Ivor Atkins had watched with interest the progress of *The Dream of Gerontius* and, sensing that, after the première, Elgar might now have some time to spare, he immediately came forward with a request for a new work for his second festival in 1902. The response was disappointing, almost to the point of being discourteous:

> Langham Hotel, Portland Place, London W.
> Tuesday p.m. (postmarked 11 December 1900)

> My dear Atkins,
> I had a letter from the Secretary of the Festival enquiring as to a new work. I had to decline, but expressed a hope for 'Gerontius'.
> I also recommended strongly Walford Davies. I hope you approve of this and will back it up. I think he ought to have a chance; don't you?
> Kindest regards to Mrs Atkins and yourself.
> Yours ever,
> Edward Elgar. [69]

Naturally the events of 1901 had been dominated by the death of Queen Victoria in the January and the impending coronation of Edward VII. Almost inevitably Elgar was linked with appropriate ceremonial music for the latter: there were enquiries for a Coronation March, but Elgar withdrew from this when he discovered that other composers had also been approached, thereby creating a competitive element; there was also a suggestion for a *Coronation Ode*, to a text by Arthur C. Benson (1862-1925)[70], which the composer enthused over, completing it in time for the 1902 Coronation celebrations which, in the event, were postponed because of the King's illness. It was eventually premièred at Sheffield, and revived for the Coronation of King George V in 1911, with Elgar adding a further movement in honour of Queen Mary. This was by far the most sizeable of all Elgar's laureate works, and he was not yet Master of the King's Musick, an honour which surprisingly did not come his way until 1924. The *Coronation Ode* had to wait until the 1990 Worcester Festival[71] to receive recognition from the Three Choirs. Presumably the patriotic tones were again held against it; earthly kings should presumably not have received musical commendation under an ecclesiastical roof, although they happily figured in the official prayers.

That performance was memorable for so many things, not least the splendour of 'the famous tune' in a cathedral acoustic, with the additional trumpets ringing around the building, and the choir in resplendent tones. Many of those present were overcome with emotion, the Mayor of Worcester and his entourage delirious with excitement and waving Union flags, and even the clergy were caught up in the euphoria. Elgar would have been amazed, and thrilled. I am sure the Almighty would have smiled benignly on the proceedings, well-pleased with the genius that he had given us.

'That tune', which the King had said would travel the world, originally formed the trio section of the first *Pomp and Circumstance March*, which had been written for Elgar's friend Alfred E. Rodewald

(1861-1903)[72] and his Liverpool Orchestral Society towards the end of 1901 and, together with the second *March in A minor*, can be seen as the composer's response to the *Coronation March* project, which he had spurned. Most of the musical – and unmusical – world recognises the theme of the first march as one of the great tunes of the century; a minority consider that it debases Elgar's art. He himself had no worries about it, responding to criticism by writing:

> I have some of the soldier instinct in me and so I have written two marches of which, so far from being ashamed, I am proud. . . . I like to look on the composer's vocation as the old troubadours or bards did. In those days it was no disgrace for a man to be turned on to step in front of an army and inspire them with a song.
>
> For my part, I know that there are a lot of people who like to celebrate events with music. To these people I have given tunes. Is that wrong?[73]

Elgar's Marches have received scant recognition by the Three Choirs Festival over the years. The *Pomp and Circumstance March No. 1* was played for the first time as the recessional procession at the Opening Service of the 1981 Worcester Festival. To the surprise of the writer, who was conducting, the audience stayed standing and suddenly, led by the chorus, burst into spontaneous song at the final peroration. It seemed a perfectly natural thing to do, even at that solemn occasion, such was the hypnotic power of the piece.

This expanded mention of Elgar's ceremonial pieces merely serves to illustrate his identification with the national mood of celebration at this time, and perhaps give some extenuation for his reluctance to produce anything new for Atkins in his 'Coronation year festival'. Perhaps more importantly he viewed the prospect of a Three Choirs' presentation of *The Dream of Gerontius* as an opportunity to show the musical world that he had produced a masterpiece to rank with the greatest in the choral repertoire. The Three Choirs owed him that, and the performance promised by Atkins would be given in his beloved Worcester Cathedral, where he claimed that his music would be heard to its best advantage, for 'the building does it.'

Atkins had chosen a formidable programme for 1902, with symphonies by Beethoven, Brahms and Tschaikovsky, *Tod und Verkärung* by Richard Strauss (a Three Choirs première), a group of 'Coronation novelties', a Bach cantata, choral offerings by Granville Bantock, Horatorio Parker, the new work – *The Temple* – commissioned on Elgar's advice, from Walford Davies (1869-1941), the traditional *Elijah* and *Messiah,* and, of course, *The Dream of Gerontius.* All this had to be rehearsed in the two London days with the orchestra, and on the grim Monday combined rehearsal in the Cathedral; this was also the first year in which the responsibility for the chorus was placed wholly in the hands of the local singers. Tough demands were made on these singers for, not only did they have to overcome the complexities of *The Dream of Gerontiu*s which had so puzzled their Birmingham counterparts, but they also had to contend with some extremely awkward writing by Walford Davies, whose work and personality did not endear him to either choir or orchestra. Elgar's generosity to a young composer appeared to be less shrewd on this occasion, yet Walford Davies did figure in the programmes for several years afterwards, and there is little evidence to suggest that his music was anything less than effective, and sometimes innovative.

Naturally Elgar, with his newly-acquired fame, was the celebrity of the Festival, and his residence for the week – Castle House in College Green – was the scene of much coming and going of distinguished musicians and friends; everyone wanted to be seen in his company. In some ways this Festival was the last in which he would be the 'local boy made good'; from now onwards he would be gracing the Festival with his presence as an established international artist. He appeared on the rostrum for his *Sursum Corda* at the Opening Service, at the secular concert for the *Cockaigne Overture* and three songs from the *Sea Pictures*, sung by Muriel Foster, replacing the indisposed Marie Brema, who was to have sung two songs by Saint-Saëns; there was also the first Three Choirs' hearing of his arrangement of *God save the King*, which had been written earlier in the year. But it was *The Dream of Gerontius* which was eagerly awaited, and when Elgar stepped on to the podium that memorable Thursday evening, the Cathedral was full to overflowing with more than three thousand listeners. It was the first performance to be conducted by the composer.

But the path to performance had not been an easy one and, for once, it was not the performers providing the problems. The text was always likely to be a stumbling block to Anglican sensibilities: the references to the Virgin Mary and Joseph, to Masses, to the saints, to souls in purgatory, to say nothing of the whole concept of the poem, was considered to be alien to the Thirty-nine Articles of the Church of England. The Stewards began to have doubts.

In fairness to the Cathedral clergy, most of them were keen for the performance to take place, but approval from the Bishop was essential before the plans could go ahead. Elgar understood the difficulties well enough, accepting that a compromise was inevitable.

With the Festival deadlines drawing alarmingly close, the Elgars had taken themselves off to Germany for the Lower Rhine Festival at which *The Dream of Gerontius* would be performed. Having realised that Elgar had failed to raise the matter of changes to the text with Father William Neville, Cardinal Newman's executor and copyright owner, Atkins took the responsibility of settling the issue himself. A visit to Father Neville with two draft sets of modifications – one by the Bishop Gore of Worcester, the other by himself, based on previous discussions with Elgar – elicited a somewhat reluctant approval, but at least it seemed now that the performance plans could proceed without further doctrinal complications. The changes involved the replacement of all references to 'Mary' with 'Jesus', 'Saviour' or 'Lord'; the substitution of 'souls' for 'souls in purgatory' and 'prayers' for 'masses', and the omission of the Litany of Saints from Part I. All this was clearly unsatisfactory, but Elgar, who referred to it as 'a dreadful mix-up', accepted the situation, as his prime concern was to have the music heard in his own cathedral. However he did express some pent-up resentment in the well-known passage from a letter to Jaeger on May 9th of that year:

> The whole objection now is manufactured by one man with the express purpose of (as he thinks) ruining the work and me.

It has never been established who the one man might be, although the finger is frequently pointed at the unfortunate Stanford, but it is more likely to have been the Archbishop of Canterbury, who was even opposed to the publication of the *English Hymnal* because of its perceived Anglo-Catholic leanings.

The chorus rehearsals appeared to proceed satisfactorily, but more problems emerged as the London orchestral rehearsals drew near. The chosen tenor, William Green, had double-booked and would only be able to attend the final rehearsal in Worcester. Elgar was not happy, stressing that 'it is really absurd to think Gerontius can be whistled through like a well-known work.'[74] Atkins concurred and Green was replaced by John Coates, who was to become the first of the great tenors to be synonymous with the work. But the soloist problem did not end there, for the contralto, Marie Brema, became ill just prior to the London rehearsal, and was replaced at even shorter notice by Muriel Foster, who in any event had been one of Elgar's original suggestions for the part of the Angel. The bass was Plunket Greene. So, almost by accident, the final line-up was as fine as the composer would be likely to find from the list of established British oratorio singers. There can be no doubt that this trio of soloists were a major factor in the success of that great performance, although it was recorded that the chorus were in splendid form. Elgar himself must have been under emotional strain, as his mother had died only a week prior to the performance; to publicly mark his grief he conducted in mourning black. All these ingredients would have contributed to this deeply moving occasion, the like of which will in all probability never again be experienced. The composer, Granville Bantock[75], who was at the concert, wrote:

> Never have I experienced such an impression before, as I
> did on hearing *Gerontius* this morning in the Cathedral. If
> Elgar never writes another note of music, I will say that he
> is a giant, and overtops us all. His music moved me
> profoundly. . . . It is a great work, and the man who wrote it

is a Master and a Leader. We were all deeply affected and
gave way to our feelings. While Elgar was conducting, the
tears were running down his cheeks. I want to hear nothing
better.[76]

The press were unanimous in their praise of the work and its
performance, although some poured out vitriol on the clergy for their
narrow-mindedness on the text. *The Musical Times* suggested that it 'had
been purposely mutilated to suit Anglican tastes', and *The Daily
Telegraph* critic summed up the opinions of most people when he
commented that 'surely it is time for the cathedral clergy to recognize that
if a work of art cannot be performed in its integrity it should not be
produced at all. . . . Great is the mystery of godliness.'

It was inevitable that this historic performance would overshadow
the remainder of the Festival programme, but some other interesting facts
are worth noting. There was a generous gesture by Ivor Atkins to his
predecessor, Hugh Blair, to première his cantata *Song of Deborah and
Barak*, although it nearly did not happen, due to the late arrival of the
parts. Again, Elgar helped an old friend in need, for, apart from almost
certainly recommending the work in the first place, he undertook most of
the scoring when the composer was clearly under strain to complete the
cantata in time. The work, which was said to contain 'much scholarly and
effective writing' satisfied the critics well enough. Another significant
work in the programme was the *Stabat Mater* by Dvořák, the composer
who had been such a major influence over the young Elgar, when he had
played under his baton at the 1884 Festival; but now both occupied an
equally honoured place in the programme and, if anything, the younger
man had taken over at the top of the league table of living composers - at

least in Britain. It remains to mention one more point before we take leave of this momentous Festival: playing in the back desk of the festival orchestra was one W.H. Reed[77], who would soon move through the ranks to become the leader of the London Symphony Orchestra and to enjoy a close friendship with the composer.

The Worcester achievement with *The Dream of Gerontius* heralded a whole series of successful performances around the country (nor should we forget the famous performances in Germany, which established Elgar's reputation abroad); the Birmingham débâcle had been erased from the memory of all but those who had experienced it at first hand. Fame for the composer was now a reality, bringing with it a succession of concert invitations as well as commissions. Leeds was tentatively accepted for 1904, when a Symphony was again mentioned as a possibility, but first there was the Birmingham promise to be fulfilled. Work had begun again on the *The Apostles* project, but, though the composer had stated that it would be even finer than *Gerontius*, there was little evidence of this on paper with less than a year to the date of the première. But the subject had been exercising the composer's mind almost since childhood and, from early 1903, he gave the project his almost undivided attention; some of the thematic material was culled from earlier works and sketches, but is no less effective for that and, anyway, Elgar was always something of a magpie.

The conception and construction of this gigantic work are a subject too complex and extended to be discussed here, beyond the remarkable fact that Elgar himself compiled the text for this, and its companion work *The Kingdom*. He consulted Roman Catholic and Anglican friends, and made a special study of *The Divine Tragedy* by his favourite poet, Longfellow; but, in the final reckoning, Elgar took personal responsibility for the sequence of events portrayed in the text of the oratorios. The great scheme, in the manner of Wagner's *Der Ring des Nibelungen*, would comprise a trilogy of oratorios on the subject of the Apostles, Jesus and the Church, and the Last Judgement. The leitmotif formula, adopted from Wagner and used to good effect in *The Dream of Gerontius*, would provide various threads through the trilogy, creating a group of choral works entirely new in concept to the British musical public, who were steeped in a traditional oratorio method as exemplified by *Elijah* and the like. Naturally *Gerontius* would have provided enough hints of what might be expected, but the style had not yet been attempted successfully on a Biblical text.

Elgar's previous oratorios and major cantatas had always featured a character in an heroic mould, who was supported by a 'motherly' figure: for *The Apostles* it would seem that the heroic figure could be Peter, the founder of the Church, but the two characters that dominate are surprisingly the converted Mary Magdalene, who was given almost heroine status in the Longfellow poem, and the betrayer Judas Iscariot, for whom Elgar creates a most powerful role. The compilation of the text is masterly, and this time there would be no doubting from the Anglican clergy, even if the Judas section occasionally – in Elgar's own assessment – borders on blasphemy.

Unable to complete his original scheme for the first oratorio of the trilogy because of time and ill health, together with the acceptance of numerous conducting and concert engagements, Elgar decided to curtail the project, ending at the Ascension scene. In fact there was already two hours of music, so any more would have made it unwieldy in a concert situation; but a more effective culmination of the work could not be imagined. The final pages are equal to, if not better, than any peroration by Mahler or others of the high romantic period, and in the opinion of many are among the most inspired that Elgar ever wrote.

The scoring of *The Apostles* was completed in mid-August, in time for the 1903 Festival at Hereford. The Elgars took a house for the festival week, inviting Rodewald and Schuster[78] to stay with them, but inevitably there would be a host of welcome visitors. There was even time for a private run-through of *The Apostles*, with John Coates singing the role of John. Naturally Elgar's own music was featured in the programme: he conducted the *Enigma Variations* at the secular concert, and his *Te Deum* and *Benedictus* were again sung at the Opening Service, but it was *The Dream of Gerontius* that would again be the highlight of the Festival. Once more attracting a huge audience, the work was this time sung without textural revisions, a huge plus-mark for the Hereford clergy, and, in company with *Elijah* and *Messiah*, was now classified as 'one of the pillars of the Charity'.[79]

Although he had lost some of his initial enthusiasm for the work of Coleridge-Taylor, mainly as a result of his suspicion of the unprecedented popularity of the *Hiawatha* sequence, Elgar was still gratified to find the younger composer featured in the programme with his cantata *The Atonement* – a Festival commission. He was also fascinated to hear *A Christmas Mystery (Ein Weihnachtsmysterium)* by the German composer Philipp Wolfrum (1854-1919), who had conducted several first performances in Germany of Elgar's works. In the event, both cantatas proved to be disappointing, but it must have been difficult to compete with the euphoria surrounding the Elgar masterpiece.

The Birmingham performance of *The Apostles*, conducted by the composer, was a triumph, and the critics were generally profuse in their praise and admiration for the work and its composer/conductor, although some had reservations about the incomplete nature of the project. Joseph Bennett was again in the vanguard of those who predicted a great future for the work, writing:

> The occasion may be described as in some respects unique. It was so in my own personal experience, for through all the years in which I have known the Birmingham Festival it has never happened that the whole musical world, not only in this country but also abroad, has gathered more or less closely around the production of an Englishman. It is a good omen that at last a man of our own race and nation has come to the extreme front, and drawn to himself the wondering admiration of all who profess and call themselves musicians and lovers of the art. . . . There must be something in him much more than common to bring about this result.[80]

The Apostles was a perfect work for the Three Choirs, and Brewer was quick to seize upon the opportunity of including it in his outline programme for Gloucester in 1904. Moreover, as the Dean Spence-Jones, described as 'that staunch friend of the Festival' remained opposed to *The Dream of Gerontius* in any form, it meant that, for the first time at a Gloucester Festival, Brewer was able to present a full-scale work by Elgar.

Exhausted after his work on *The Apostles*, Elgar was now faced with pressure from Leeds for completion of their commission, but his new thinking was not for another choral work, as he was anxious to pay a tribute in the form of a symphony to Dr Hans Richter (1843-1916)[81], the conductor who had championed his works. But neither project went forward at that time, as the year had ended in sadness with the sudden death of his friend, Rodewald, a loss which greatly affected Edward, who persuaded Alice to accompany him to Italy for a protracted holiday, in the hope that he could recover from the stresses of the previous months, and perhaps recapture his inspiration. They returned home in early February, in order to prepare for the Covent Garden Elgar Festival, which would be attended by the King and Queen, and for which Edward was completing an Overture. Back in Worcestershire the Elgars were faced with the expiry of their lease on the house in Malvern and, having found a residence of distinction in Hereford, decided to move to that 'sweet borderland' where Alice predicted 'Elgar would write great music'. She was absolutely right.

By the time of the Three Choirs Festival, its own son would be made a knight of the realm, Elgar's name appearing in the King's Birthday Honours list announced on 23rd June; so to Gloucester went the honour of being the first to welcome Sir Edward Elgar among its list of composers and conductors. The Tuesday evening programme began with the *Prelude* and *Angel's Farewell* from *Gerontius*, and the newly-composed *Overture 'In the South'*[82] was conducted by the composer at the secular concert, 'breathing the warm sunshine of Italy' into the proceedings. The interest for *The Apostles* resembled that for *The Dream of Gerontius* in the two previous festivals, the attendance easily exceeding that for the two standard works at the beginning and end of the week. A magnificent team of soloists had been engaged: Madame Albani, Muriel Foster, John Coates, Frangcon-Davies, Dalton Baker and Plunket Greene, the first four named having been involved in the work's première at Birmingham. This was clearly a work which would be relished by performers and audiences alike at the Three Choirs, receiving the rare distinction of being presented at four consecutive festivals. Another much smaller Elgar offering to that Gloucester Festival was the provision of a cadenza for the third movement of an Organ Concerto by a former Gloucester organist, Charles Harford Lloyd (1849-1919)[83], as an anonymous gesture of friendship.

The remainder of 1904 was not particularly fruitful in terms of composition for, not only had he withdrawn from the Leeds commission, but Elgar was occupying much of his time enjoying the fruits of his previous labours by travelling around the country conducting or listening to his works – and, no doubt, he was tinkering with sketches for the forthcoming symphony and the next oratorio of the trilogy. The only work to be completed that autumn was a third *Pomp and Circumstance March*, which he dedicated to Ivor Atkins. He continued to pick up doctorates from a galaxy of universities, and was almost persuaded to accept the inaugural Chair of Music at the new University of Leeds; however, he did eventually succumb to pressure from the University of Birmingham to occupy a similar post there, an appointment which in time would cause him much grief, for academic requirements were not his style. Much more agreeable would be his involvement with the London Symphony Orchestra, which was beginning to evolve at this time: for them, and at the request of Jaeger, he completed the *Introduction and Allegro*, a work which he had been working at since 1901, but it was considered a failure at its first performance.

With the Three Choirs returning to Worcester in 1905, Atkins made overtures to Elgar to serve on the festival executive committee, which, after some subtle persuasion, he agreed to do. At an executive meeting in January Atkins was invited to write a short choral work for the festival and immediately approached Elgar to assist in compiling a suitable libretto. The text duly arrived by the end of April and Atkins set to work with great enthusiasm. The result is a splendidly wrought work, rewarding to sing, and to play. Inevitably it was heavily influenced by Elgar, especially in the orchestral scoring, with which, as Atkins became busier with festival matters, he had given a helping hand.

The final programme for 1905 resembles an Elgar Festival, for more than a quarter of it was devoted to the music of the local 'distinguished citizen.' It was also the occasion of the composer receiving the Freedom of the City of Worcester, an honour which gave him the greatest satisfaction of all those being heaped upon him. The ceremony was conducted in the Guildhall prior to the Tuesday morning Concert, at which Ivor Atkins would conduct *The Dream of Gerontius*, the oratorio taking over the traditional place of Elijah in the programme timetable. The text was the same as that used at the 1902 performance. Appropriately this was followed by the première of Atkins' new work, *Hymn of Faith*. Elgar was on the podium to conduct *The Apostles* in the Cathedral, and the *Introduction and Allegro* at the Public Hall. The Elgars again stayed at Castle House for the week, acting hosts to several close friends, including Schuster and Jaeger, the latter showing signs of a worrying illness. Immediately following the Festival the Elgars set out for a cruise in the Mediterranean, not returning home until mid-October. Composition had been seriously neglected so far in a year which had already included an extended first visit to America, but now Elgar was obliged to turn his attention to another Birmingham Festival commission, the result of which would be the sequel to *The Apostles*.

Much of the material was to hand, together with an outline of the libretto, but another vast canvas was envisaged which would necessitate months of intense work. As with *The Apostles*, the length of the work was subsequently adjusted to conform to a normal concert duration. The chosen title was *The Kingdom*, continuing the story of the Apostles and the establishment of the Church in Jerusalem. In this context the role of Peter assumes more heroic proportions, and the consoling presence of Mary pervades much of the work, her famous Soliloquy moving Elgar to new heights of inspiration. The work, more concise, less dramatic, and a perfect contrast to the earlier oratorio, is described by Jaeger[84] as the 'purest and serenest of all the composer's works, with its elevating message of spiritual peace and comfort.'

Much of 1906, except when on trips abroad, was spent working against deadlines, and the scoring of *The Kingdom* had only been completed just prior to the Hereford Festival. Although a house party had been arranged at their own home for festival week, Elgar himself was so engrossed with checking orchestral material that he only attended the Festival to conduct his *Introduction and Allegro* at the secular concert, leaving the direction of *Gerontius* and *The Apostles* in the capable hands of Sinclair. Ten years had elapsed since he had been so little involved in the Festival, even though he was now a resident of the host city, but his music was there to speak strongly for him.

All attention was now centred on the eagerly-awaited new work at Birmingham, and the public were not to be disappointed. The first performance in Birmingham Town Hall on 3rd October was conducted by Elgar with Agnes Nicholls, Muriel Foster, John Coates and William Higley as soloists. There was a huge attendance, with a considerable number of people standing; leading musicians were there from all over Britain, such was the magnetism of an Elgar première. It was an event to savour, and the critics – with the exception of Ernest Newman – were ecstatic. The *Birmingham Daily Post* reported that 'it testified to the popularity of the great English composer, the man of the hour, who has instituted a new art form in oratorio', while *The Birmingham Mail* commented on a more personal element when writing 'Sir Edward Elgar's emotions were so stirred by his own wonderful work that, according to the observation of the choristers, tears were streaming down his face several times during the oratorio.'[85]

Although Elgar toyed with the idea of a third oratorio – indeed some of it had been written – it never came to fruition. His last oratorio had been written, and he was about to enter into a short unprofitable period as far as major works were concerned. But a symphony was brewing up inside him, if only to prove to the bigots that the art was not dead when produced by the hands of genius. In the meantime here was another work which had all the right ingredients for success at the Three Choirs. *The Apostles* and *The Kingdom*, which had been performed on consecutive days at the Birmingham Festival, were to become staple fare in the Three Choirs programme, the only regrets being that they had not received their first performances at the event, for surely Elgar had the festival in mind when writing them? He would have known only too well how the Three Choirs would relish these works; they cry out for that special cathedral atmosphere. Indeed the critic, Ferruccio Bonavia (1877-1950)[86], wrote that 'except at the Three Choirs Festivals, we have never heard a performance of this work (*The Apostles*) that could be called adequate, while some performances, even conducted by Elgar himself, fell far short of mere adequacy. It was pitiful to see him sometimes conduct forces utterly incapable of doing justice to his music or to his direction.'[87] At the Three Choirs the public and performers knew Elgar well, understanding his music and his personality; in spite of the derogatory remarks that he was wont to make, he knew in his heart that this was where he belonged.

The three conductors of the festival had probably long since given up any hope of Elgar fulfilling a commission for them, and had to rely on any scraps which might fall from the master's table. No such scraps were needed for Gloucester in 1907, the year of the composer's fiftieth birthday. Brewer seized upon the opportunity of repeating the Birmingham formula of presenting the two great oratorios on successive days, *The Apostles* on the Tuesday evening and *The Kingdom* on the following morning, a unique happening in the history of the Three Choirs Festival. This pattern was to be repeated again in Elgar's lifetime – at Gloucester in 1922, and Worcester in 1926 – but it was not until the 1984 anniversary year at Worcester that the works were presented on the same day, posthumously fulfilling one of Elgar's wishes. *The Annals of the Three Choirs* noted that 'large audiences assembled to listen to the touching strains of Sir Edward Elgar's music. A dignified and reverential performance of the exalted theme was given under the composer's direction.' The inclusion of the two oratorios, understandably the only Elgar works featured during the week, provided something of a 'get-out clause' for the Gloucester committee, who were still obliged to ignore *The Dream of Gerontius*, due to the stubbornness of the Dean. How long could they continue to hold out against public opinion?

It was a lean year for composition, the only works of consequence to appear being the first *Wand of Youth Suite*, a collection of picturesque pieces drawn from early workings for a children's play, and the fourth *Pomp and Circumstance March*, dedicated to Sinclair. Both works were immediately seized upon by British orchestras.

The travelling and guest conducting continued unabated, another Leeds Festival commission had been turned down, and a decision had been made to abandon the third part of the projected trilogy; his attention was at last turning towards a symphony. The sketches were now building up, but in between all this he wrote many of his finest and most challenging partsongs, many of them inspired by the rising political worries in Europe and the need for a renewal of nationalism; this latter mood was to be incorporated into the 'scherzo' movement of the forthcoming symphony. A six months sojourn in Italy had not really produced the stimulus that he needed, and he returned to his Hereford home fairly empty handed as far as the symphony was concerned. But, back in his natural environment, the muse was activated, and the *Symphony in A flat* was completed within a space of three months, receiving its first peformance under Richter on 7th December at the Queen's Hall. This was the work that the world had been waiting for. It was immediately recognised as one of the pinnacles of achievement in this form, receiving over a hundred performances in its first year. It is interesting to note that Mahler's equally portentous *Symphony No 8*, written in the previous year, was not to receive its première until two years later, and then in a foreign country.

From the beginning of that momentous year Elgar and Atkins had been conducting a correspondence regarding the forthcoming 1908 Worcester Festival. Elgar endeavoured to persuade Atkins to add 'new blood' to the list of artists engaged for the festival, but expressed some concern at the inclusion of a violinist in the Cathedral programme on the grounds that it could introduce a secular atmosphere! Hints for a new work and a subsequent formal invitation inevitably fell on stony ground, but the draft programme did include a repeat of the Gloucester experiment of the two oratorios on consecutive days. This plan was rejected at a later meeting of the executive committee in favour of the inclusion of *Gerontius* for *The Apostles*. Elgar wrote to Atkins from Rome:

Suite No. 2, "The Wand of Youth" (Op. 16).

EDWARD ELGAR.

(Music to a Child's Play).

I.   March.

II.   The Little Bells (Scherzino).

III.   Moths and Butterflies.

IV.   Fountain Dance.

V.   The Tame Bear.

VI.   The Wild Bears.

The pieces are a second and final portion of the music intended to accompany an unacted play devised long ago.   The "drama" was commenced in 1869, and the music underwent rearrangement and received additions for several years.

The circumstances, which gave rise to the little allegory set forth in the play, passed away, and with it the play also disappeared.

But the music remained; some numbers were completed (e.g., No. 3 of the present suite), while others existed only in sketches.   During the last year the orchestration has been revised and some of the movements re-written, but the main features remain as in the original.

During an enforced rest from larger and more complicated work it has been an amusement to reconstruct and rehabilitate these pieces which now obtain their first performance not far from the place of their inception.

Elgar's programme note for the première of 'The Wand of Youth Suite, No. 2' –
Worcester 1908.

> I fear I cannot write anything new. I make a suggestion with much fear and trembling and you must please decide whichever way you think..I have the *second Suite* UNHEARD from the *'Wand of Youth'*. If you think it would be any sort of popular attraction I would conduct it at the Concert.

Not surprisingly Atkins accepted this offer with alacrity, even if the work was hardly likely to be seen as a major contribution to the history of the Three Choirs. Nevertheless Elgar's note on the work makes for interesting reading, establishing a convincing argument for its first performance in his home environment. The performance itself received a tremendous ovation from a packed audience, who demanded a repeat of the last two movements.

Atkins conducted *The Dream of Gerontius* on the Tuesday evening, and the next morning, with Sir Edward at the helm, Worcester was given its first hearing of *The Kingdom*. It proved to be a memorable performance and, at the moment of the Lord's Prayer, the whole audience stood in silence, although the *Yorkshire Post* suggested that the performers had 'little feeling for the words'. The same report questioned the doctrinal prejudice in the continued use of the bowdlerised version of *Gerontius*, pointing out that 'the prayers for the Blessed Virgin Mary not allowed on Tuesday evening will be permitted on Thursday morning when Stanford's *Stabat Mater* will be given. This, however, will be under the discreet veil of the Latin language'.[88] Sadly it was noted that there were many empty seats for the performances of both Elgar oratorios. At the Opening Service Atkins had included the orchestration of Bach's *Toccata in F* by Heinrich Esser (1818-1872), but was unhappy with the effect of the ending; Elgar readily agreed to his request to re-orchestrate this part of the work, clearly enjoying the task. Atkins suggested that Elgar might be interested to orchestrate the *Prelude and Fugue in E minor* (known as *The Wedge*), a piece which meant a lot to both musicians; it will be remembered that Elgar had been fascinated with it on hearing it played by S.S. Wesley at the 'Mock Festival' in 1875. Regrettably Elgar never did get round to this task, so we can only imagine what he might have done with it.

The Elgars' large house party that year was accommodated at the King's School House, which lacked some of the customer comforts of their previous residences, particularly the ability to summon up the domestic staff, so Edward organised a system of individual sounds for each guest. The situation is admirably described by Billy Reed:

> Sir Edward at once saw his chance and took it. He set off to the local toyshop and bought up everything that would produce an individual sound. Then he drew up a scheme for the various bedrooms . . . and hung up the list in the kitchen. He told me it was worth waking up early in the morning to hear Mrs Worthington appeal plaintively on the penny whistle from her door, or Frankie Schuster blow a fanfare on the tin trumpet from his, or three or four of them together set up a din which only the trained ear could disentangle.[89]

This is just an indication of the great satisfaction and joy that Elgar derived from these sociable occasions, serving to remind us that he was capable of radiating fun, a factor which was not often evident in his music. He was the master of what he termed 'the jape', that old English

WORCESTER FESTIVAL, 1911.

SIDE SHOWS

(By permission of Mr. Queer Hardie, M.P., and in Contemptuous Defiance of the Dean and Chapter).

Monday, 12th September, LECTURE in the Commandery by the O.M., entitled:

" Dyspeptic Hagiology Biologically Considered and Quantitatively Analysed."

Lie-m-Light Illustrations.

"Advertising Quartets" by the Beecham Guinea Orchestra of Coloured Specialists and the Holloway Knockabouts.

Tuesday, 13th September. Popular Day.

BURNING OF HERETICS

(Supply not guaranteed; every endeavour will be made to procure fresh imitations).

FREQUENT PARACHUTE DESCENTS

from the Cathedral Tower by Mrs. Worthington and the Trombones of the Orchestra.

SUMMER SPORTS in the Close (conducted by Dr. Elizabeth Pastoral).

STRIKE MEETING of Composers for a Four-hours' Day and a British Pitch.

MOONLIGHT ASSAULT on the Elgar Tower by the Blacklegs of the Close.

Thereafter minions will raise " L " to the B(d)gar Statue.

Wednesday, 13th September.

GREAT ARSON ACT.

Firing of a Nunnery previously selected by a Committee of blinded Early Perp. Experts. The O.M. will fire the first faggot at Curfew.

Thursday, 14th September.

MIRACULOUS INTERLUDE

Miss Grafton (from Italy, where she has been studying the Science) will sail in a stone coffin (courteously provided by Canon Wilson, who will later on perish at the stake) from the Bridge to the Ferry. *En route* she will jerk a miracle selected by the Commissary of Oaths from a richly-assorted and old-landed parcel. The O.M., dibbling from the stern of the cist with a pig-tailed worm will repeatedly hook poly-carp, laughing daces, and gold-ring-containing perch, thereby administering a considerable slosh in the jaw to St. Mungo, who is expected to be present and make a few remarks for publication (or otherwise).

Friday, 15th September.

GRAND CONCLUDING ECCLESIASTICAL SCENA.

The Bishop of the Diocese, seizing the opportunity to procure a residence in the City, will (preceded by his Examining Chaplain) enter a newly-excavated Bear Pit in College Yard. Buns will be retailed by the Dean and Members of the Chapter at an easy rate.

CONCLUDING FIREWORK DISPLAY by the Minor Canons, Composers, and Prophets.

LEICESTER, TYP., WORCESTER

Parody programme compiled by Elgar for the 1911 Festival

expression for a joke or prank and, when the festival came round to Hereford in 1909, his most mischievous trick to date concerned an invitation to a party on the last evening of the festival. A large gathering of friends found Elgar in his most relaxed and hilarious mood at the party held at Harley House, which the Elgars had taken for the week in view of Carice's quarantine for scarlet fever.

1909 was the year of the *First Symphony*, with performances all over the country. Inevitably it was included in the Hereford programme, with the composer conducting, although, in an odd piece of programme planning, it was followed by J.S. Bach's motet *Be not afraid!* The programme for the week also included *The Apostles*, the *Te Deum*, and the first performance of *Go, song of Mine*. This miniature had been written when the Elgars had been on holiday in Italy earlier in the year. Inspired by a visit to St Mark's, Venice, and touched by the recent death of his trusted and valued friend, Jaeger, he produced his most elaborate essay in partsong form in this setting of a poem by the medieval Italian poet Cavalcanti, translated by Dante Gabriel Rossetti. It is of some significance that this work, called a chorus – for it is neither a partsong nor a motet – has the same key as the *Violin Concerto*, and has all the hallmarks of his mature style. The Three Choirs had regularly included an unaccompanied work in its programme, usually an inflated piece of church music or, worse still, an indiscreet performance of a Renaissance masterpiece; but the musical public saw it as an indispensable part of the festival fare, and loved it. What they really thought of this new Elgar work is not documented, especially as it was sandwiched between Parry's *Job* and Part One of Haydn's *Creation,* but it is certain that they were unknowingly witnessing a masterpiece. It may last for only five minutes, but contains as much concentrated emotion as any of Elgar's major works. It demands supreme skill from the singers (the chorus range is one of four octaves), but the effect is stunning when the piece is sung well. How the singers at that first performance coped with its intricacies must be open to some doubt, especially as the chorus singing was not rated too highly by the critics at that festival. The secular concert, which included the Overture *Cockaigne,* had the added interest of an appearance of Frederick Delius to conduct his *Dance Rhapsody.* Little could he have imagined that one day his choral music would be heard in a cathedral setting, although that would not be until nearly forty years after his death.

Through most of 1910 Elgar was working at the *Violin Concerto*, as well as coming to terms with the *Second Symphony*, a project with which he had been wrestling for some time. It was the former which was completed first, and there was a memorable moment at that year's Gloucester Festival when at the house that the Elgar's had rented – this time at the Cookery School – there had been a rehearsal of the *Concerto* with Kreisler[90], to whom the work is dedicated, and who was the distinguished guest soloist at the Festival. This was followed later in the week by an 'official' run-through before invited guests. Earlier in the festival there had been the much documented 'private' hearing, before an invited group of friends, by Billy Reed, leader of the Festival Orchestra for the first time, who wrote:

> I must confess I had some inward qualms. I knew every note of the concerto, and exactly how he liked it played: every nuance, every shade of expression; yet I felt a little overwhelmed at being asked to play the solo part at what would be the very first performance before an audience. It was one of those facts that you cannot annihilate by just

> calling it private. Nearly all the prominent musicians
> engaged at the Festival were there . . . some of the musical
> critics and the house-party. The room was full; and all the
> lights were turned out except for some strange device
> arranged by Frank Schuster for lighting the piano and the
> violin stand.[91]

These private hearings were to bear fruit at the Worcester Festival the following year, but Elgar's involvement with Gloucester was to conduct the *First Symphony,* (surrounded in the Wednesday programme by a bizarre collection of pieces by Parry, Basil Harwood, C. Lee Williams and Hermann Goetz (1840-1876), all of which received accolades from the press) and, for the first time at Gloucester, *The Dream of Gerontius.* The Dean and Chapter had at last withdrawn their embargo, but still insisted on Anglican correctness of text. As a sort of overture to the oratorio there was a new work by a 'fairly unknown West Country composer', Ralph Vaughan Williams. That work was, in its own way, to become just as celebrated as Elgar's oratorio: the *Fantasia on a theme of Thomas Tallis.*

Atkins had signified his intentions of including Bach's *St Matthew Passion* in his 1911 programme but, dissatisfied with the existing English edition, set about the task of preparing a new edition which would reflect a closer attention to the original score in respect of text underlay and other detail. Towards the end of 1910 he managed to enlist Elgar's help in the project, the agreement being that Atkins would concentrate on the words, while Elgar would bear responsibility for the music.

In some ways it was surprising that Elgar agreed to undertake this task as, not only did he still have a heavy concert schedule, but he was now fully immersed in the completion of the *Second Symphony*. It was also Coronation year, and he was expected to write a March and an Anthem for the ceremonies in June. Atkins continued his work on the *St Matthew Passion* unaided, but made every effort to involve a reluctant Elgar. In the event he contributed enough to warrant sharing the editorial credits on the title page of the publication, just in time for the Festival preparations.

The new edition was performed at the Thursday morning concert of the Festival[92], attracting much attention, not least because of the novelty of a chorale being played by a brass ensemble from the top of the cathedral tower before each part of the work. The idea of this came from Atkins, who had experienced something similar on a visit to the walled town of Rothenburg ob der Tauber. A request to Elgar to orchestrate the chorales met with a positive response, but expressing doubt that the players would respond: 'they will expect a holiday' wrote the composer. However, having enthused the brass players with the proposal of the tower music when he met them at the London rehearsals, Atkins renewed his request to Elgar to make the arrangements, and the score and parts were ready for the players when they arrived in Worcester for the festival. The effect was described as 'sensational', Robert Buckley writing: 'Aloft, out of sight, a hundred and seventy feet in the air, the brass of the orchestra gave forth the old German chorales harmonised by Bach two centuries ago. They rang out over the College Green, those perfect harmonies, over the city, over the river, the meadows, and the hills.'[93] The Chorales were played at each performance of the *St Matthew Passion* up to the time of the second World War, but their revival at Worcester in 1978 proved to be something of a disappointment as a result of increased traffic noise.

*The brass arrangements of Chorales from Bach's 'St Matthew Passion' played,
not from the tower, but from the South Porch of Gloucester Cathedral – 1913.*

Another feature of that 1911 *St Matthew Passion* performance was the playing of the violin obbligato by Fritz Kreisler in the solo *Have mercy*. Kreisler was at the Festival to play the first Three Choirs performance of Elgar's *Violin Concerto*, a momentous event during that week, as well as in the history of the festival. The *Concerto* was preceded by the première of Vaughan Williams' *Five Mystical Songs*, and there is the story of the composer, while conducting his work, being shocked to see Kreisler playing in the back desk of the violins; the maestro was merely 'warming-up' for the next piece!

Go, song of mine, a great favourite of Atkins, was included in the Tuesday evening 'Coronation' programme, although on this occasion it was listed as a Motet, a term which Elgar disliked, but he also found 'Chorus' a dull description. The matter of a suitable definition for this work has never really been resolved. At the Wednesday secular concert Elgar conducted his new *Coronation March* in a programme which also included two of the *Sea Pictures*, but the principal Elgar interest of the week centred around the *Second Symphony*, which the composer conducted in the Cathedral earlier that day.

In a year that had promised so much for Elgar - and he was elated to receive the Order of Merit in the Coronation Honours List – he was devastated to feel that his new Symphony, first played in London on May 24, had not been received with the same enthusiasm as his other recent works. The mood appeared too sombre for a musical public brought up on pageantry and the good things of life; they were unable to understand the darker tones of this new masterpiece. Dwindling attendances for the Symphony at London and other performances were offset to a certain extent by the vast audience that assembled to hear the work at Worcester and who, by all accounts, gave the work a sympathetic hearing.

There was the usual house-party, this time happily back in Castle House, and it found Elgar in his most festive spirit. His latest jape was a handbill announcing a series of side-shows to take place during the festival week. This fascinating document alludes to various festival personalities, as well as national figures,[94] and makes amusing reading even without knowledge of the fictional participants or events.

By the first days of the new year the Elgars had moved from Hereford to the first house that they had ever owned, Severn House at Hampstead. The house promised much, but Edward became very unwell with a mysterious illness that laid him low for several months. All this delayed his work on another Birmingham commission for the autumn of 1912, although he was enthusiastic about writing incidental music for a patriotic masque, *The Crown of India*, celebrating the Indian Coronation of the new King George V and Queen Mary. For this he raided many of his earlier works and, following the successful first performance in March, he set about preparing an orchestral suite from the existing score. This would receive its first public performance at the Hereford Festival secular concert.

As his health gradually improved, so Elgar began to work seriously at the new Birmingham work, together with a 'big' anthem – a setting of Psalm 48, *Great is the Lord*, and the Symphonic Study, *Falstaff.* All this was combined with his new activity as principal conductor of the London Symphony Orchestra, succeeding Richter, who had retired at the end of the concert season.

That year's Hereford Festival contained several Elgar novelties for, in addition to *The Crown of India Suite*, two of his songs - *The Torch* and *The River* – sung by Muriel Foster (her last festival) were heard in orchestral garb for the first time, and the *Coronation March* was played at the Opening Service. *The Dream of Gerontius* was back in the programme, conducted by the composer, and featuring for the first time at a Three Choirs the tenor, Gervase Elwes, arguably the finest interpreter of the principal role. The critics enthused over this performance, even though it was still hampered by the textural restrictions, the *Annals* noting that 'well over two thousand attentive listeners assembled to hear this pathetic work'. We would probably expect rather different phraseology today! And there was also the *St Matthew Passion* in the Elgar/Atkins edition, complete with tower music. There was no house party for this festival, the Elgars preferring to stay the week at the Castle Pool Hotel, which was near enough to the centre of social activity. An interesting feature of the programme that week was that Walford Davies failed to complete his commission for the Festival, so his projected work was replaced by Schubert's *Unfinished Symphony*!

The Birmingham work turned out to be a setting of Arthur O'Shaughnessy's poem, *The Music Makers*. Here again Elgar delved back into his earlier works to provide expression for the poem's imagery, but the fusion of all this material with his new writing is eminently successful, producing a work which tells us all that we would ever want to now about the man and his music. This auto-biographical essay is a choralist's dream, containing some of the composer's finest writing for voices. It is a greatly underrated and sadly neglected work. The first performance at Birmingham on 1st October, 1912, was reported to have been very fine, with the chorus in great form, but the work itself was viewed with some suspicion. The self-quotations were considered to be a particular weakness, and this period of 'dreaming' was clearly not understood by those who still associated Elgar with the triumphant voice of the *First Symphony* or the romantic outpourings of the *Violin*

Concerto. Elgar sums up this period of his compositions in a letter to Mrs Stuart-Wortley[95], which states: 'I have written out my soul in the concerto, Symphony II and the Ode and you know it . . . in these three works I have shown myself.'

The Music Makers was not immediately taken up by the Three Choirs for, again, there was some suspicion of the text, and clergy permission had to be sought before it was eventually passed fit for ecclesiastical consumption in time for the 1920 Festival. It was said that the mention of God in the text swayed the balance in its favour!

Also on Elgar's drawing board at this time was the Symphonic Study, *Falstaff,* the composition of which was said to bring him 'a great deal of happiness'. Again working from earlier sketches he created a programmatic work to compare with anything produced by Richard Strauss or Liszt, and which was to be his last major purely orchestral work. This stunning musical portrait of the Shakespearean complex character was first heard at the Leeds Festival on 1st October, 1913. It was always to be an unlikely work to figure in a cathedral concert, but it is surprising that it never appeared at a secular concert; indeed, it was not heard at all at a Three Choirs until Gloucester 1989.[96]

In between the premières of these two great works came the Gloucester Festival of 1913, when Elgar conducted his *Second Symphony* and *The Dream of Gerontius*. The *Coronation March* was again played at the Opening Service, and, for the third year in succession, the *St Matthew Passion* - and the tower music - was given. Elgar's position was somewhat over-shadowed at this Festival by the appearance of Camille Saint-Saëns (1835-1921) , who conducted his new oratorio *The Promised Land*, and featured as soloist in a Mozart Piano Concerto. No other celebrated European composer had figured in the Three Choirs programme since the visit of Dvořák in 1884, but Saint-Saëns was no threat to Elgar's reputation, as the oratorio proved to be something of a non-event.

Before the year was out Atkins was again exercising his powers of persuasion on Elgar for a new work at the Worcester Festival of 1914, and for a time there seemed to be a glimmer of hope - even Part III of the *Apostles* sequence came into the reckoning. But it all came to nothing, and by February Elgar was suggesting that he might 'find some new short thing'. This must have been very frustrating for Atkins, especially when he ascertained that Elgar was now seriously considering Part III of the trilogy for another friend, Henry Charles Embleton (1854 - 1930)[97], in the hope that the work would be premièred at Leeds. Resigned to yet another disappointment, Atkins planned a programme in which Elgar would still be featured strongly. Of course there be would *Gerontius*, hopefully conducted by the composer, and there was also the possibility of *Falstaff*; the newly-composed anthem *Give unto the Lord*[98] was pencilled in for the Opening Service, together with the now almost obligatory *Coronation March*. In the event plans were changed, and the anthem was dropped from the scheme, (and so was *Falstaff* in favour of the *Introduction and Allegro for Strings*), but a Grand Closing Service was planned, in which Elgar's other large-scale anthem, *Great is the Lord* would be featured.

Elgar was not pleased, writing to Atkins:

> I have been rushed to a great extent or I should have written
> at once to say I do not understand on what ground you have
> withdrawn the anthem at the opening service. I have been
> wondering if I am really wanted at all, but I hesitate to
> withdraw entirely from the festival although there is no

inducement for me to come: you see Gerontius 'goes' without me. . . . So do not announce anything conducted by me for the present and I will see.[99]

But all this was academic. The war that had been threatening for some time eventually broke out and, after a short period of postponement, the executive committee, at the end of September, decided to abandon the Festival until further notice. So the Three Choirs Festival fell silent for the first time in two hundred years. When it returned – if it returned – the world would be a very different place, the ambience of the Festival would have changed, and Elgar's role in it would be substantially different. Sadly, the vintage years were over.

Worcester Musical Festival,

September 6th, 8th, 9th, 10th and 11th, 1914.

THE 191st MEETING OF THE THREE CHOIRS OF WORCESTER, HEREFORD AND GLOUCESTER.

Principal Performers:

Madame NOORDEWIER-REDDINGIUS.
Miss DOROTHY SILK.
Miss CARRIE TUBB.
Miss RUTH VINCENT.
Madame KIRKBY LUNN.
Madame DE HAAN-MANIFARGES.
Miss SARA SILVERS.

Mr. JOHN COATES.
Mr. GERVASE ELWES.
Mr. STEUART WILSON.
Mr. HERBERT HEYNER.
Mr. CHARLES MOTT.
Mr. ROBERT RADFORD.

ORGAN, Mornings - - - Dr. A. H. BREWER.
„ Evenings - - - Dr. G. R. SINCLAIR.

Conductor: Mr. IVOR ATKINS.

IN THE CATHEDRAL.

Sunday, Sept. 6th, 3.30 p.m.   GRAND OPENING SERVICE, WITH CHORUS AND ORCHESTRA.

Tuesday Morning -
Sept. 8th, 11.30 a.m.

Gerontius - - - - - - - *Elgar*
Three 8-part Motets for unaccompanied Chorus
(Fest- und Gedenksprüche) - - - *Brahms*
Symphony in D Minor - - - - *Franck*

Tuesday Evening -
7.30 p.m.

Elijah - - - - - - *Mendelssohn*

Wednesday Morning
Sept. 9th, 11.30 a.m.

Manzoni Requiem - - - - - *Verdi*
Fantasy (founded on passages in Dante's
Divina Commedia) (New work) - *Walford Davies*
Blest Pair of Sirens - - - - *Parry*
Motet for unaccompanied Chorus - *Orlando di Lasso*
Symphonic Poem, "Tod und Verklärung" - *Strauss*

Thursday Morning -
Sept. 10th, 11.30 a.m.

Mass in B minor - - - - - *Bach*

Thursday Evening -
7.30 p.m.

Symphony in G minor - - - - *Mozart*
New Work - - - - *A. E. Brent Smith*
New Work - - - - *Vaughan Williams*
Creation, Part 1 - - - - - *Haydn*

Friday Morning - -
Sept. 11th, 11.30 a.m.

Messiah - - - - - - - *Handel*

Friday Evening, 6.0 p.m.   Closing Service by the Three Choirs.

IN THE PUBLIC HALL.

Wednesday Evening
8 p.m.

Concert. "Till Eulenspiegel" - - - *Strauss*
and new works by *Elgar, Sibelius,* etc.

*Programmes with all information as to Tickets, etc., may be obtained from
Messrs. Deighton & Co. and Messrs. Spark & Co., Worcester.*

CHORUS AND ORCHESTRA OF ABOUT 400 PERFORMERS.

Reduced Railway Fares from nearly all parts on production of **Festival Ticket.**

All Seats are Numbered and Reserved.   Prices from 2/6 to 15/-.

The draft programme for the abandoned Festival at Worcester – 1914.

Elgar chats with the Prime Minister, Stanley Baldwin;
Ivor Atkins watches approvingly.

4

The Emeritus Years

'I have been thinking so much of our lost Festivals - no more music. . . . Everything good and nice and clean and fresh and sweet is far away, never to return.'[100]

The Festivals did return, but Elgar's world would be vastly changed. So many friends and acquaintances had failed to come back from the conflict; Sinclair of Hereford had died suddenly in the February of 1917 and the death of Parry shortly before the Armistice in 1918 affected Elgar deeply. But the greatest blow to the composer was imminent – a setback from which he would never recover: Alice's health had become a matter of great concern, and she died on the 7th April, 1920, just four months before the revival of the Festival at Worcester. His desolation and loneliness became unfathomable, and it was inevitable that Atkins' request for a short new work for the revived 1920 Festival would be declined. A long letter to Atkins[101] expressed a hope for *Gerontius* and the *Music Makers* in the programme, together with a preference for the *Second Symphony*, if such a work was being considered. There was a suggestion that a civic procession with doctors of music and the military wearing suitable robes would look splendid, but the letter also contained the poignant paragraph: 'I am sorry, sorry to be so unhelpful. We had been looking forward to the dear old festival and suddenly the whole thing is hurled away from me.'

In truth the old festival very nearly did expire, for there appeared to be little local enthusiasm for a revival, and music making of this sort, with its social overtones, did not figure greatly in people's minds in those post war years. It was the persistence of Ivor Atkins that won the day. For many months he canvassed his plans, encountering much apathy, and even some doubts from Elgar, who questioned the financial viability of staging a revival at this point in time; but a standing committee, which met in the November of 1919, agreed to a festival the following year, subject to various financial conditions. There were the usual objections to the erection of a platform and charge for admission to the concerts, but after much hard work and determination, together with support from civic and church leaders, Atkins achieved his goal; by early June the programme had been finalised, and the requisite number of stewards had been assembled to ensure financial stability.

The *Annals* noted the meeting of old friends, and the 'constantly expressed sympathy for those (and alas! they are many) who sang and played in 1913 at Gloucester and have since made the great sacrifice'. The resuscitation of the festival against all the odds brought the comment that 'all feel and rejoice that the storms that once threatened to wreck the ship have been safely weathered'.[102]

The sun shone throughout this wonderful week, which apparently found all participants in good form; there seemed to be a new spirit abroad. But the sadness of the recent turmoil and the absence of devoted festival musicians and patrons inevitably cast its shadow over much of the programme. Sullivan's *In Memoriam Overture* was played at the Opening Service in remembrance of Dr Sinclair, and musical tributes were paid later in the week to other notable festival musicians, such as Parry and Harford Lloyd. Elgar's *Music Makers*, heard at a Three Choirs for the first time, seemed especially appropriate, the final phrases of 'a singer who sings no more' having a profound effect on all attending that concert, which appropriately included Atkins' *Hymn of Faith*, a work which may well have had an influence on Elgar as he prepared his Ode for, although a much larger-scale work, it employs the same forces. The soloist on this occasion was the much-admired Astra Desmond, making her dèbut at the Three Choirs. Emotions were to be stirred even more at the Thursday evening concert when Elgar conducted his setting of Laurence Binyon's poem, *For the Fallen*, a work which seemed to express so perfectly the mood of national mourning and regret. *For the Fallen* is the third movement of *The Spirit of England*[103], Elgar's only major composition from the war years. It was also to be his last choral work, the complete cycle receiving its first performance in London on 24th November, 1917. The whole work is inscribed 'To the memory of our glorious men, with a special thought for the Worcesters.' The writing displays a continuation of the 'heroic melancholy' which had been experienced in the *Second Symphony* and the *Music Makers,* and which was to find its zenith in the *'Cello Concerto*, completed two years later.

The Dream of Gerontius (still governed by Anglican correctness) occupied its expected place in the programme, and replacing the hoped for symphony in the secular programme was the *Introduction and Allegro for Strings.* The latter was included in a programme which featured other local composers, both of whom had been encouraged by Elgar: Alexander Brent Smith[104] (*Worcestershire Rhapsody*) and Julius Harrison[105] (*A Worcestershire Suite*). The remainder of the programme that week contained the expected *Elijah, Hymn of Praise, St Matthew Passion* (complete with the tower Chorales) and *Messiah*[106] to round off the week. The Three Choirs Festival was back on course, but its future would have to be considered very carefully, for musical fashions and tastes had changed dramatically. It might survive in its old format, but it would also need to retain and strengthen its Elgar association. Whether Elgar himself felt this bond and shared this responsibility is another matter.

For this festival Elgar had lodged quietly with Carice at his Uncle Henry's old rooms in College Precincts. Little was seen of him socially, and he found solace in playing cribbage or walking along the river bank with Billy Reed. Following the Festival he had written to Reed that 'your presence and help made all the difference to me . . . if you had not been there – you knew my dear wife so well – I don't think I could have borne it.' He later wrote to Alice Stuart-Wortley: 'I like to think of Worcester days and you and the flowers and the fruit and the warm sun and my cathedral and the music: but it *is* lonely.' His appearance on the podium and the music which he conducted gave the appearance of autumnal lamentation; he felt he was a relic of a previous age, his music having no place in a post-war generation. He turned away from works on a large canvas, like other great composers finding satisfaction in the personal utterances of chamber music. The 'Brinkwells period'[107] had inspired the creation of the three great chamber works, the *Violin Sonata*, the *String Quartet* and the *Piano Quintet*[108], but arguably the greatest work to come from that time of sadness and melancholy was the *'Cello Concerto*.

Elgar was also concerned at the arrival on the scene of Bartók, Schoenberg, Stravinsky, and others, who he felt were threatening the very foundations of all that was respectable in musical creation. Schoenberg had created a new dodecaphonic – or twelve-note – system of composition, which was to have a dramatic effect on Western music for the next fifty years or so. The choice facing composers at the beginning of the 1920s was to find a new way of designing their music or somehow to refurbish past conventions. Elgar had no heart for this new thinking; he would have shared the view of Serge Prokofiev (1891-1953) that 'music has definitely reached and passed the greatest degree of discord and complexity that can be attained in practice.'[109] His depressing view of the future of English music was largely governed by his own experiences, for – except at the Three Choirs – his music was experiencing a decline in public interest. Even the première of the 'Cello Concerto at the Queen's Hall, London on 27th October, 1919, had failed to attract attention, with a sparsely-filled hall; to make matters worse the work had been under-rehearsed, and its mood misunderstood, resulting in a deplorable performance. At least Ernest Newman, writing in *The Observer*, recognised the Concerto's merits, while berating the orchestra for making 'so lamentable a public exhibition of itself.'[110]

Hereford 1921 would be the first festival to be conducted by Percy Hull, who had become a close friend of the composer. He had been interned by the Germans while on a walking tour in 1914 and, following the death of Sinclair in 1917, Elgar made every effort to encourage the Dean and Chapter to suspend an appointment of a successor until Hull had returned.

In a letter to Hull he had written: 'We will welcome you home again with enthusiasm and I trust the post of organist in your own cathedral will be yours. I was only too glad to do what I could to further your claims.' Elgar and other supporters had their way, and Hull was duly appointed on his return at the end of 1918. His first festival was awaited eagerly, and it follows that Elgar would figure prominently in the programme plans. *The Apostles* was the principal work of the Wednesday morning concert, and

The Dream of Gerontius occupied what was fast becoming its traditional 'slot' on the Thursday evening, although still not allowed to stand on its own. On this occasion it was prefaced by a charming, but fairly lightweight, Christmas Hymn *Before the paling of the stars* by Benjamin Dale (1885-1943). Contemporary reports suggested that both Elgar works were finely performed, the *Annals* making the quaint remark that 'once again the music (*Gerontius*) in its impressive surroundings produced that wholly religious effect which presumably the composer intended it should do', rather suggesting that, even after twenty years, the work remained something of a mystery. But the principal Elgar interest at this festival centred on the playing of the *'Cello Concerto* by Beatrice Harrison at the secular concert, a performance which brought much acclaim, and went a long way towards erasing the memory of that dire first performance in London. The traditional Hereford Chamber Concert produced another Three Choirs première: Elgar's *Piano Quintet* played by the W.H. Reed String Quartet, with Dr Henry Ley[111] (1887-1962) at the piano.

Elgar continued to give encouragement to other composers and, on this occasion, he persuaded Hull to programme *The Hymn of Jesus*[112] by Gustav Holst (1874-1934). Elgar and Holst were never more than casual acquaintances and, in truth, did not care much for each other's music, although Holst was always grateful to Elgar for raising hopes of an English musical renaissance. It is surprising that Holst was never accepted as a 'Three Choirs composer', although *The Hymn of Jesus* has appeared at regular intervals, and a couple of shorter works received premières at Gloucester between the wars.

In preparation for the 1922 Gloucester Festival Brewer sought the advice of Elgar on the matter of commissions to suitable younger composers. Elgar's recommendations were Arthur Bliss (1891-1975), Eugène Goosens (1893-1962) and Herbert Howells (1892-1983), all of whom would 'do away with the notion that everything must be a sort of Church of England propaganda.'[113] The most substantial work of the three turned out to be the *Colour Symphony* by Bliss, but apparently Elgar did not like its early Stravinskyan overtones, and must have made this known to the composer, for relationships were strained for several years because of Elgar's 'biting tongue, which on one occasion hurt me very much'.[114] In the same programme was *Silence*, a setting by Goosens of a Walter de la Mare poem. Elgar's views on this work are less clear, although neither received encouraging critical reviews, even the normally docile *Annals* stating that the two compositions 'contained such terribly harsh progressions and positively ugly idioms of the ultra modern school, that opinions were freely expressed about the propriety of admitting such music into the programme for the Cathedral, where at any rate we may hope and expect to be edified by music suitable to the solemn and mysterious atmosphere of religious exaltation.' It stands to reason that Elgar, having proposed these composers, would be less than enchanted by the reception that their works received, whatever his own personal views might have been. Perhaps it should be mentioned that this extremely challenging programme began with the controversial *Le Poème de l'Extase* by Alexander Skryabin (1872-1915), which, while now recognised as a significant work of its time, would have made an uneasy impression with the traditional festival-goer; the young composers with their new works would have faced an already alientated audience – they could not win!

The new piece by Howells – *Sine Nomine (A Phantasy)* – was placed before Mendelssohn's *Elijah* at the opening concert, an astonishing

Gloucester Festival, 1922
following the unveiling of the Parry Memorial
standing (left to right): Brewer, Sir Hugh Allen, Granville Bantock, Sir Henry Hadow
seated (left to right): Elgar, Bishop Gibson, Lord Gladstone, Dean Gee, Stanford

Gloucester Festival, 1922
(left to right): Arthur Bliss, Herbert Brewer, Billy Reed, Elgar, Eugène Goosens

misjudgement of programme planning resulting in another unfavourable audience reaction, which was almost certainly responsible for the fact that this complex impressionistic work was not heard again until its second performance at a Gloucester festival seventy years later. There is a touching story of Elgar, sensing that the young conductor/composer was becoming increasingly harassed at the final rehearsal, offering time that he had been allocated for his own *Gerontius* rehearsal. Howells never forgot this generosity.

The Gloucester sensitivity to the *Gerontius* text may have been the reason for that work's exclusion from the scheme, but this omission was redressed by the programming of *The Apostles* and *The Kingdom* on consecutive days, with Elgar conducting – a repeat of the Gloucester initiative of 1907. Elgar was also featured in the Thursday evening programme when he conducted *For the Fallen* and his transcription of J.S. Bach's *Fantasia and Fugue in C minor*, of which the *Fantasia* was receiving its first performance. The transcription had come about as a result of an agreement made at a lunch meeting in London with Richard Strauss (1864-1949). After discussing the orchestration of Bach's organ music, Strauss promised to transcribe the *Fantasia* if Elgar would take responsibility for the Fugue. Elgar completed the orchestration of the Fugue quite quickly, and with enthusiasm, but Strauss failed with his part of the bargain; so, a year later, the Fantasia was finished in time for inclusion of the complete work at the festival. It was a bold move of Elgar to present a baroque work in this inflated guise, for the movement towards authenticity had begun, and neo-classicism was now a powerful voice. Inevitably it suffered somewhat at the hands of the critics, but the orchestration is absolutely sumptuous. In a letter to Goosens, Elgar had written: 'I wanted to show how gorgeous and great and brilliant Bach would have made his music sound if he had had our means.' This was the first of a series of arrangements and transcriptions with which, in the absence of any new works from the master, the Three Choirs would have to content itself over the remaining years.

By this time Elgar was beginning to overcome his grief, gradually entering more into the spirit of festivity; by 1923 he was back to his exuberant best at house parties, with Billy Reed always at his side to encourage and enliven him. Although he was still subject to black moods, Elgar certainly seemed to have renewed vigour and interest, especially after he had moved back to Worcestershire, but the hoped-for new work (perhaps the third part of the *Apostles* trilogy) would never appear at a Three Choirs. Worcester 1923 would have to be content with a galaxy of arrangements and orchestrations.

A piece which had fascinated Elgar for many years was the Overture to Handel's Second Chandos Anthem, which he had known in an old organ arrangement. Early in 1923 he decided to orchestrate it in 'epic' style, and subsequently offered it to Atkins for the festival, where, as the *Overture in D minor*, it was first heard at the Opening Service. Like the Bach transcription, it makes a most satisfying 'filler', but it has always been more widely used than the earlier arrangement; for some reason it seems more respectable to meddle with Handel's music!

For some months Elgar had endeavoured to persuade Ivor Atkins to compose a new piece for this festival, but it did not materialise, so an existing work – the anthem *Abide with me* – was suggested for the Opening Service. Atkins was also reluctant about this proposal, as he was too busy to undertake the necessary orchestration; with his usual generosity, Elgar offered to do it for him, and the scoring was completed in a couple of weeks. This was clearly an exercise which afforded him great pleasure and satisfaction and, at Atkins' request, he also undertook the orchestration of two anthems – *Let us lift up our heart* by S.S. Wesley, a cantata-style work which had so impressed him at the 1875 Festival, (and which was a particular favourite of Atkins), and a beautiful penitential anthem *O Lord, look down from heaven* by the Georgian composer Jonathan Battishill (1738-1801) – one of the gems of English Cathedral Music. It is hoped that one day these orchestrations will turn up. Their complete disappearance would be a tragic loss, for they represent an important part of Elgar's creative life. A recording of the complete Elgar transcriptions and arrangements used at the Three Choirs would be a most interesting and valuable project. But where are the scores of these anthem transcriptions?

The rest of the week rather resembled an Elgar Festival; indeed this was really the pattern of these Meetings for the remainder of the composer's life. On this occasion he conducted *The Dream of Gerontius*, *The Kingdom* and *For the Fallen* in the Cathedral, and Beatrice Harrison was engaged again to play the *'Cello Concerto* at the Public Hall. The records tell us that no less than twenty-one British composers were represented during this week, including Arnold Bax (1883-1953), Gustav Holst and Ralph Vaughan Williams (1872-1958), but clearly Elgar was not much impressed with their music for, after the Festival, he wrote to Alice Stuart-Wortley: '*The Kingdom, Gerontius* and *For the Fallen* are not bad; I think I deserve my peerage now when these are compared with the new works!!!'

At a special ceremony during the Festival Elgar unveiled a window to the memory of five former cathedral organists buried in the cloisters; in every way he was now the Festival celebrity, although he chose to ignore the fact. In private he had regained much of his former ebullience and affection, but outwardly he still chose to present a more severe face, claiming to be disenchanted with music and the world in general. But when on the podium, conducting in court dress or the robes of one of his multi-array of doctorates, all was forgotten and forgiven; he really was 'the star of the show'. The eminent critic of the *Manchester Guardian,* Samuel Langford (1863-1927) summed it up beautifully when he wrote in 1922 that 'the true revelation of Elgar's music has been found not everywhere in England, but is bound up with certain golden days of autumn when, sitting in the cathedrals of Worcester, Gloucester and Hereford, we have heard Elgar at work.'

And so the 'show' moved on to Hereford in 1924, by which time Elgar had been appointed Master of the King's Musick, a role which he had effectively been fulfilling in all but title for over twenty years. His first official appearance in this capacity was at the Wembley Exhibition in July of 1924, and for which he wrote the *Pageant of Empire,* a cycle of eight movements to words by Alfred Noyes (1880-1959). He had previously written an *Empire March* for the same ceremony, and this was played at the Opening Service of Percy Hull's second festival.

The Elgar offerings in the programme were almost identical with the previous year at Worcester, even to the repeat of two of the Opening Service arrangements, showing a certain lack of enterprise as well as a curious neglect of the major orchestral works, none of which had received a hearing since before the war. Bach, Handel and Mendelssohn occupied their usual places in the programme, and there was a 'remarkable rendering' of Brahms' *Requiem.* A musical tribute was offered to the memory of Parratt[115], Bridge[116] and Elgar's old adversary, Stanford, all of whom had died earlier in the year, but the remainder of the programme included an assortment of minor pieces by lesser composers, that in some ways demeaned the status of the festival, returning to the excesses and banalities of the previous century. Writing a few years later, C.W. Orr (1893-1976)[117], assessing this period of Elgar's life, comments:

> . . . it is scarcely an exaggeration to say that Elgar has shown himself like some 'sea-shouldering whale' among the little dolphins and porpoises who have floundered uncomfortably in his immense wake. And what is the most gratifying thing to record is that the general public seems at long last to have recognised him for what he is. After some of the Symphonic Depressions of our younger men his music comes like a health-giving tonic. . . It is becoming more and more evident that he, who has never worried about 'nationalism', is the most national of all our composers. His music could have been written only by an Englishman, and that is one reason why English audiences should understand him best.[118]

This so admirably sums up what the Three Choirs audiences had known and appreciated for many years.

In November of that year Elgar received from Schuster the news that Gabriel Fauré had died, which saddened him greatly for he had much affection for the Frenchman, who he described as 'a real gentleman'. He immediately promised to do everything that he could to bring Fauré's music to the attention of the English musical public, beginning by suggesting to Brewer that he should present the British première of the exquisite *Requiem* at the 1925 Festival. Amazingly, the idea was dismissed as being too great a box-office risk and, in spite of Elgar's continued championship of the work, it was not heard at a Three Choirs until four years after his death – at Worcester in 1938.

In general Gloucester adopted a safer policy of programming and commissioning in 1925: the novelties on offer, 'so eminently suited to the Three Choirs'[119], were by more established composers who would be unlikely to ruffle the die-hard feathers of the stewards. Naturally Elgar was there to conduct *The Apostles* and *For the Fallen*, and the *First Symphony* was heard again at a festival after a lapse of fifteen years. Nothing of Elgar was included in the secular concert at the Shire Hall, an occasion which heralded the arrival of broadcasting at Three Choirs 'since thousands of people all over the British Isles and beyond were listening to it by wireless, via London.'[120] What we now take for granted must have been the cause of great excitement, for this was the medium by which the festival would be taken out of its perceived provincial limitations; that Elgar was not a part of this new venture was a mystery, for surely he would have added credibility to what was otherwise a fairly mundane programme, judged by our contemporary observations. The records were also pleased to note 'the novelty' of the first appearance at a festival of a lady composer/conductor in Dame Ethel Smyth (1858-1944).

Elgar's health had deteriorated through 1925, culminating in an operation at South Bank Nursing Home in Worcester over the Christmas period. As soon as he seemed well enough Atkins began discussing plans with him for the 1926 Worcester Festival. In the first exchange of letters Elgar wrote:

> I have been thinking over the 'scheme' and my brains do
> not envisage any 'draw' amongst the classics. I *wish* you

could get some *decent* Bach instead of the infernally dull
(some of them) cantatas; if we had anyone to sing them! it
would be different, but the miserable *yowling* we get
wearies me.

Do not forget Mozart, Schubert . . . How about the evening
concert or concerts? Shall you have the small orchestra
again in College Hall? I hope so and *do* knock out that
awful woman who mis-sang with pianoforte!'[121]

Over the next couple of months letters and discussions between the
two centred on the possibility of taking up the offer from HMV to record
performances at the Festival. By this time Elgar was completely
infatuated with the whole aspect of recording, but his enthusiasm was not
shared by Atkins or the executive committee. There were fears that such
a recording might prejudice the attendance at concerts, as well as
reflecting adversely on the festival's reputation if the performances
happened to be below the expected standard. In the event any clash of
interest was eliminated when the project foundered over a problematical
contractual arrangement with the London Symphony Orchestra.

Naturally there was still hope for a new work from Elgar's pen, and
for a time he did work at some sketches for *Apostles III*, but, as always,
it came to nothing. However he did agree to write an orchestral suite
based on the incidental music that he had composed for Laurence
Binyon's play, *King Arthur*, in 1923; this would be the centre-piece of the
concert in College Hall on the final night of the Festival. Although the
work had not been mentioned for several months, Atkins took the liberty
of including it in his draft programme, which he sent to Elgar for
approval. It came back with the *Suite* crossed out, and the appended

words 'Alas! No'. So once again Worcester would not have a new Elgar work – nor even a transcription. In fact he applied his pen to no work of any sort during 1926.

The *Annals* for that Festival make extraordinary reading, especially the following paragraph:

> It was the writer's good fortune for a few years to live within hail of Worcester and to note how three performances attracted the agricultural attention and interest more than anything else. The opening Orchestral Sunday Service, the *Elijah*, and the *Messiah*. Fathers, mothers and children were to be seen heading for the Cathedral in all sorts of conveyances and many on foot, leaving hops, turnips, and barley to take care of themselves for a few hours of 'jolly fine music.' Let the musical authorities note these things and not scare away, by too many experiments in modern music, the love of the lowly for Handel, Haydn, Mozart and Mendelssohn which still exists.

This extraordinary statement goes some way towards understanding the mentality of the locals who had cast aside Elgar into the musical wilderness some forty years earlier. There would certainly be little to offend the 'lowly' audience in this programme, which was fairly conventional, allowing for the fact that Elgar would now be considered almost on a par with the quartet of composers mentioned above. He was naturally well-represented with performances of the *Enigma Variations* (the first time since 1903), *For the Fallen* and, yet again the Handel and

Battishill transcriptions at the Opening Service. *Dream Children*, the delightful miniature composed in 1902, was substituted for the uncompleted *King Arthur Suite* at the Friday secular concert, although the composer declined the offer to conduct it, saying that he had 'no recollection of them – or it.' But he did direct authoritative performances of *The Apostles* and *The Kingdom* on consecutive days, the only time that this pattern had been adopted at Worcester. The usual bevy of inoffensive novelties appeared through the week, mostly at the secular concert, but one highlight was surely the first Three Choirs performance of a symphony by the now-established Vaughan Williams (although the final movement of the *Sea Symphony* had been permitted at Gloucester the previous year); he conducted his *Symphony No 3 – The Pastoral*, presumably included to satisfy the bucolics! Elgar's relationship with Vaughan Williams at this time was rather tenuous, and at times the older man resorted to rudeness. But as the years passed he grew to respect Vaughan Williams' work, even if he did not wholly approve of his modal idiom, and he latterly took the younger composer under his wing, bringing him into the coterie of his closest friends.

Elgar was always on a short fuse and he reacted angrily to one of the Cathedral Canons who had made a public protest at the inclusion of a section from Wagner's *Parsifal* at this Festival. The Canon's main objection was that Wagner was a 'sensualist'; Elgar's reaction was immediate and angry, writing to the press:

> The Canon quotes 'His emotions and spiritual experiences were those of the ordinary sensual man.' But 'Aren't we all?' If the Canon really believes that such emotions in early life debar a man from taking part in the services of the

church in riper years he should at once resign his canonry and any other spiritual offices he is paid to hold.'[122]

The Canon made a perfunctory reply, but Elgar was satisfied that he had made his point. One is caused to wonder what either of them would have made of current programming which allows for such works as Carl Orff's *Carmina Burana*, or even the complete Act I of *Parsifal*, which was acclaimed as the highlight of the 1998 Festival at Gloucester?

Perhaps it should be mentioned here that Elgar generally waived his conducting fees at Three Choirs but, on this occasion, the Festival having shown a good profit, Atkins insisted that he received some remuneration. The amusing response was:

> Many thanks for the unexpected: the formal receipt accompanies this. Three tails wagged (profusely) at the sight of the cheque and the owner's prophesied *Bones*.[123]

1927, the year of Elgar's seventieth birthday, would be Hereford's turn. It would also be the year that the media arrived at the festival for, not only were the Opening Service and the first half of the Wednesday evening broadcast on the national network, but the HMV mobile recording unit was in attendance for the week to record a selection of Elgar's performances. After the disappointment of the recording project at Worcester the previous year, Elgar was delighted to find that Percy Hull shared his enthusiasm, and even a suspicious Dean and Chapter were prepared to turn a blind eye to the arrangements. As the London Symphony Orchestra were now out of contract with the rival recording company, the last obstacle had been removed. The plans were to record

Mobile recording unit at the West End of Hereford Cathedral – 1927

Herbert Sumsion – Gloucester 1928

the Opening Service, excerpts from *The Dream of Gerontius, The Music Makers*, and Holst's *Hymn of Jesus*, conducted by Hull.

For the Opening Service Elgar had specially written a *Civic Fanfare* to accompany the procession of the civic party and leading to the National Anthem. At the appointed time Elgar appeared on the podium and began conducting the world première of his new piece, only to find that the civic party had not appeared – so all had to be repeated, causing panic among the broadcasting and recording engineers; but the event was successfully recorded, even if the tonal levels left a lot to be desired. At the end of the week no less than twenty-five sides had been made from three festival performances, but a large number of the 'takes' proved to be very unsatisfactory, and there was a danger that many would be destroyed. Gaisberg[124], with Elgar's support, put an embargo on the destruction of the matrices and waxes, so that the enterprise was not a total failure. The re-mastered set of Elgar recordings, including those from Hereford, will be familiar enough to Elgarians, and are extremely valuable in giving a clear insight into the composer's interpretations. The dubious quality of the actual recordings are obvious enough, but it is the poor standard of the performers that causes the greatest disappointment and surprise. If this was the standard that regularly confronted Elgar on the Three Choirs rostrum, his frequent tantrums can be understood only too well. Atkins was obviously shrewd enough to suspect this the previous year.

This particular festival was probably the most Elgar-orientated to date for, in addition to his music at the Opening Service, there were the performances already mentioned of the *Dream of Gerontius* and *The Music Makers*, together with the *Second Symphony* (last heard at Gloucester in 1913), the *Violin Concerto* (previously given at Worcester in 1911), with Albert Sammons as soloist, and the *Overture 'Cockaigne'*. Even allowing for the silent war years the neglect of Elgar's major orchestral works at Three Choirs is hard to comprehend, and there were many of his non-choral works still awaiting a hearing in these revered surroundings. The remainder of the programme followed traditional lines, but it is interesting to observe the rising prominence of Vaughan Williams, who was perhaps being groomed as the natural successor to Elgar as the Festival luminary.

Interest then turned to Gloucester for 1928, where it was anticipated that Brewer would again present an enterprising programme; but tragedy struck when he died suddenly in early March, with the festival preparations about to get under way. The Dean and Chapter made a quick appointment, offering the post to Herbert Sumsion (1899-1995), who was working in America. Like Brewer he had been a chorister, and pupil-assistant, before searching experience in London and Philadelphia. Ironically Sumsion had just accepted the post of organist at Coventry Cathedral when the Gloucester vacancy occurred, but he was released from this commitment at the request of the Gloucester Chapter. Although fairly inexperienced as a conductor, 'John' Sumsion (as he was known to friends) made a great success of his first festival, prompting the famous remark from Elgar that 'what at the beginning of the week was an assumption is now a certainty!' Elgar was quick to welcome the Sumsions into his circle, and John became one of his most effective interpreters. It was often said that a Sumsion performance was 'as if Elgar himself had been conducting.'

The Gloucester programme that Sumsion inherited was certainly demanding, containing such works as *King David* by Honegger (1892-1955) and *Psalmus Hungaricus* by Zoltán Kodály (1882-1967), both new to Three Choirs, as well as several other unfamiliar works and the usual fare of *Elijah* and *Messiah*. But Elgar was on hand to take charge of his own works – this year *The Dream of Gerontius, The Kingdom* and the *'Cello Concerto*.

The matter of recordings had been raised again, with the assurances that the problems of Hereford would be overcome but, even after an impassioned letter from Elgar, the Dean and Chapter refused permission, apparently fearful that the operation would cause damage to the fabric and disturb normal activities. As a result of this blinkered view a unique opportunity was lost, and recordings of the Three Choirs were lost for ever, although broadcasting continued, albeit sporadically until comparatively recent times.

Immediately after the Gloucester Festival Atkins turned his attention to Worcester 1929, and a new work from Elgar was his prime objective. There was a suspicion that Elgar had regained his interest in composing, being drawn towards some poems of Shelley, but a negative response was conveyed from Dean Moore Ede, who considered the poems beautiful but pagan. He suggested that Sir Edward could find another suitable poem, as he had with Gerontius. Such hypocrisy was not lost on Elgar, who remembered only too well that for over twenty years the Anglican clergy had rejected the doctrines of his oratorio. A grumpy letter to Atkins[125] stated that 'I fear I cannot turn on another subject so easily as it seems to the Dean. Weather dull and dogs bored.' But Atkins was not deterred and he continued to pester Elgar for a new work. One letter[126] contains a particularly moving paragraph in which he pleads with the composer by writing:

> When I listen to the marvellous music that you have
> written, when I remember all that you have taught us, I

> could weep to see you keeping silence as you do. One day
> succeeds another and you will not break it. And yet I *know*
> that the old magic is there. You cannot keep back the little
> flashes that show me it is *there*. . . . Let us have the great
> days again. . . .

Shaw[127], who had in the recent years become very attached to Elgar, also tried to goad the composer into activity, but it was all to no avail. Elgar had lost interest in composition, and the only reward for Atkins' persistence was the orchestration of Henry Purcell's motet *Jehova, quam multi sunt hostes mei*. This score was in the possession of Wulstan Atkins, who gave permission for its second hearing at a concert in Worcester Cathedral in October 1995. The transcription itself showed a surprising number of errors, and there were some passages where it seemed to suggest that Elgar had lost interest, so elementary was the orchestration. It was always clear where he relished the task, especially in the declamatory passage for bass solo, and in the pentitential passages for chorus. Purcell/Elgar proves to be a most interesting and satisfying partnership.

The festival programme was again dominated by Elgar, with two oratorios, the *Introduction and Allegro*, and the *Second Symphony*, which shared the evening with Vaughan Williams' *Sancta Civitas*, a powerful work which used some of the St Augustine texts which Elgar had previously thought of incorporating into his *Apostles III (The Last Judgement)* project.

Elgar was generous in his praise of *Sancta Civitas*, accepting that he would not now be able to set those same words. Other interesting works in that festival were a *Te Deum* by the relatively unknown German

W.H. Reed, Ivor Atkins and Elgar,
prior to a Worcester Festival performance – 1929

*Ivor Atkins, Percy Hull and Herbert Sumsion
with Elgar – Hereford 1930*

composer and conductor Heinrich Kaminski (1886-1946) and J.S. Bach's *St John Passion*, performed in a new edition which had been prepared by Sir Ivor Atkins, both of which were of great interest to Elgar, who always tried to find time to listen to other works from his vantage point at the side of the platform in Worcester and Hereford, and wherever he could find a quiet spot in Gloucester. He always turned up for *Messiah*, or a part of it, an oratorio which was particularly dear to him, and had been from his youth.

For the week Elgar had rented the house Marl Bank on Rainbow Hill, a residence that he had coveted for many years, and which commanded wonderful views over Worcester towards the Malvern Hills. He purchased the house when it came on the market later in the year, the property affording him great satisfaction for his remaining years. During the Festival he entertained guests lavishly, but was also a regular visitor at other house parties, including Castle House where the Sumsions were experiencing their first 'away' social round. Elgar was always looking to join in the fun where he knew groups of musicians would be gathered.

1930 brought a spate of compositions, even if earlier sketches had been raided to complete them: the *Severn Suite* for brass band, dedicated to G. Bernard Shaw, written as the test-piece for the National Brass Band Championship, and the *Pomp and Circumstance March No 5*, which was composed for Percy Hull, but not in time for inclusion at his third Festival. Elgar was not at his best for that festival, not least because he was suffering considerable pain from an attack of lumbago. This prevented him from conducting the *Introduction and Allegro* at the Opening Service, but he was determined to take a full part in the rest of the week's activities, although he was forced to conduct seated, a source of great irritation to him; nor was he too pleased to be assisted on and off the platform, which was something of an affront to his dignity. Even with his restricted movements he still managed to procure what were considered to be fine performances of his oratorios, (this time *The Apostles* joining the ever-present *Gerontius*), together with the *Second Symphony* and the *Overture 'In the South'*. Not surprisingly Elgar appeared less friendly at this festival, claiming that he had no interest in music, insisting on being whisked away from rehearsals to the Hereford Club in order to check on the racing results, and generally being rather a bore. Yet he must surely have felt the warmth of affection from performers and audience alike whenever he took up the baton. The remainder of that year's programme contained an astonishing assortment of old, new and established works, all packed into four days, with minimal rehearsal. Some works undoubtedly suffered from scant attention, but it would be fair to say that the Elgar works were always meticulously prepared by his cathedral organist colleagues during his lifetime.

Elgar's health gradually improved, and he was elated by the reception of his *Nursery Suite*, first performed and recorded in a short space during the summer of 1931. The work was dedicated to the Duke and Duchess of York and the Princesses Elizabeth and Margaret Rose. Again he dipped into some earlier sketches for some of the material, but it was clear that he enjoyed writing once more for orchestral forces, and over the next couple of years he frequently turned his attention to the three projects that were on his drawing board – the opera, the piano concerto, and the symphony, although none of them progressed beyond a series of fragments. Sumsion held out no hope of a new work for his forthcoming 1931 Festival, which would be the first for which he had the sole responsibility of planning, but he quickly seized upon the new *Nursery Suite*, which Elgar conducted at the secular concert. Elgar was much moved by the tremendous reception which greeted the performance. The next morning he was on the rostrum in the Cathedral to conduct the *Violin Concerto*, with Albert Sammons again the soloist. Apart from some Elgar arrangements at the Opening Service, his only other work that week was *The Dream of Gerontius*, which he conducted, with Muriel Brunskill, Stuart Wilson and Harold Williams as soloists. Sumsion recalled that the rehearsal had been less than satisfactory, with Elgar displaying little interest in the proceedings. His 'jerky' beat was never easy to understand, and there was a minimum use of his normally expressive left hand, but perhaps his greatest failing from the chorus point of view was that he expected them to be on a par of attainment with the orchestra, not being prepared to give them any assistance – a dangerous practice with a largely amateur chorus; his philosophy for conducting was that the music was more important that the performers. In the actual performance of the oratorio Sumsion found it necessary to stand behind one of the great Norman pillars, out of sight of the audience, and act as a second conductor for the chorus, who were receiving no assistance at all from Elgar. But of course the strength of Elgar's performances emanated from his magnetic personality; that rare gift of being able to command respect and attention by a glance, an expression, a movement of the eyes, or just simply exuding an aura of authority by his very presence on the podium. Following that performance of *Gerontius* a critic was moved to write:

> Sir Edward Elgar conducted *The Dream of Gerontius* himself last night and again astonished us by the magic power of his personality. To listen to the sound of his own music under him is to feel that all the performers are

controlled by a great mind from the moment he raises his
baton.[128]

As he grew older Elgar was certainly prone to lose interest in a
performance if things were not going well, or if his mind was on other
matters; he was even liable to stop conducting. At one Three Choirs
performance of *The Kingdom* he became so disinterested that things
began to fall apart, and would have done so without the leadership of
Billy Reed, but, suddenly sensing the beauty of the soprano soliloquy
'The sun goeth down' (sung by Agnes Nicholls) he regained control of
himself, and brought the oratorio to a close with the utmost emotional
intensity. While he rarely lost patience with orchestral players, he
frequently crossed swords with his singers and the chorus. Lady Hull
gives a graphic description of such an occasion at a Hereford rehearsal of
The Apostles:

> Elgar walked on to the platform and took up the baton
> without even looking at the chorus, much less giving them
> a sort of greeting. He announced a number at which he
> wanted us to start in such a quiet voice that no one could
> hear him and there was an embarrassed silence . . . his
> whole manner was forbidding in the extreme . . . by this
> time the chorus was thoroughly jittery, their entries were
> tentative and, in addition to this, they began to sing flat.
> One encouraging lift of that wonderful left hand of his
> would perhaps have saved the situation, but none came . . .
> he walked off saying 'You don't appear to know anything
> of the work'. [129]

But the chorus still adored him!

The 1932 Festival once more saw Elgar on home territory. Atkins again kept Elgar fully informed of his programme intentions, and was delighted when he decided to arrange his *Severn Suite* for full orchestra, offering the first performance to the Festival. In fact the work was recorded in the April, but the discs were not issued until later in the year, so Atkins could genuinely announce an Elgar première in his programme.

Elgar agreed to conduct his own works which, apart from the *Severn Suite*, were to be *The Dream of Gerontius, The Music Makers*, the *First Symphony*, and *For the Fallen*. The last named would be sharing the programme with the young William Walton (1902-1983), whose *Belshazzar's Feast* had taken the choral world by storm at the previous year's Leeds Festival. The work to be heard at this festival was the beautiful *Viola Concerto*. Elgar made the acquaintance of Walton, conversing mainly about horse-racing, but making it clear that he had little time for his music! However, works in the programme which did give Elgar pleasure were the new *Magnificat* by Vaughan Williams, and the British première of a *Stabat Mater* by the Polish composer, Karol Szymanowski (1882-1937) – a work which has appeared regularly at Worcester festivals since. The *Piano Quintet* did make one of its rare appearances in the programme, played by the Griller Quartet with Myra Hess at the piano, although Elgar was unconcerned about its performance, claiming to have forgotten about it. 'Let it go!' he wrote to Atkins.[130]

It was noted by several listeners that Elgar's tempi appeared to be more deliberate at this Festival, the critic Bonavia noting that 'his tempi became distinctly slower and the leisurely pace brought out the charm of gracious detail with new and enchanting effect.'[131] In fact throughout his life Elgar frequently changed the tempi and negotiated his own special brand of rubato, depending on conditions, his emotional state, and the forces in front of him; the other performance details were clear enough in the score for all to observe. No other composer ever gave such clear and profuse instructions on the printed page, the sadness being that so often, then and even now, so many of these directions were and are ignored.

Throughout the Festival Elgar appeared to be in fine form. He entertained a large house-party at Marl Bank, and kept 'open house' between afternoon and evening performances. Indeed he was the 'life and soul of the party' wherever he went, appearing at most events through a hectic week and displaying energies which belied his seventy-five years. He was always immaculately dressed, usually in a white summer suit, and conducted himself with a military gait, even though his worrying 'sciatica' now caused him to use a walking-stick for support. Among friends he was jovial and affectionate; to strangers he could still appear shy and aloof, as befitting a person of such deep sensitivity. Wulstan Atkins noted that for the *Messiah* he sat in his steward's seat with Carice and the Shaws. 'It was one of the few occasions on which I saw him sitting throughout a performance.'[132]

The question of the new Symphony was on everyone's lips during Festival week, and tentative questions were put to Elgar, none eliciting a positive response. A constant companion through the week was a young violinist from the orchestra, Vera Hockman, with whom Elgar shared a love of poetry. As she bid farewell to Elgar at the end of the Festival he presented her with a copy of *The Music Makers*; written on the title page, and underlined, he had written:

> A singer who sings no more.
> i.e. Edward Elgar.

Elgar with Dr. Herbert Brewer – Gloucester 1925

Dr. Percy Hull with Sir Edward Elgar, O.M. – Hereford 1933

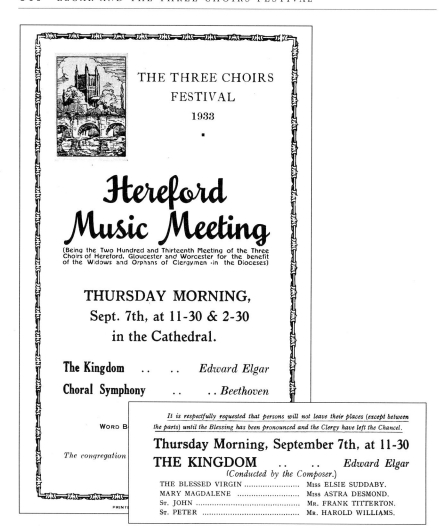

Extracts from the 1933 Hereford Festival Programme –
documenting Elgar's last appearance on the rostrum

So attention now turned to Hereford, where Percy Hull was again preparing a most interesting programme for the 1933 Festival. There would be a veritable feast of Elgar, even though it had something of a valedictory look about it. Elgar had had a busy year, and his health was obviously failing, but he looked forward to Hereford, taking up residence for the week at The Priory, a house with a most attractive garden. The weather was brilliant, and Elgar enjoyed having 'open house' to his regular visitors, many hours being spent relishing the splendour of the garden. He still presented a suave image with his stylish 'county' mode of dress, together with his impeccable formal attire on the platform, but it was noticed that he did not appear so much at the traditional parties, that he tired so easily, and experienced difficulty in walking. Conversation too became more nostalgic than usual, and he talked freely and profoundly about other composers and their music. But, once on the rostrum, he shed all his weariness and, if anything, his charisma and dynamism seemed stronger than ever.

He certainly took on a huge burden for an ailing person. There was the *Civic Fanfare* and the *Triumphal March* from *Caractacus* at the Opening Service (the latter transposed into B flat to fit the key of the music around it), a very moving performance of *The Dream of Gerontius* with soloists Astra Desmond, Frank Titterton and Horace Stevens and, at the Wednesday evening concert, the *Concerto in E minor*, performed by Lionel Tertis, who had made the arrangement for Viola, with the composer's enthusiastic permission. But the climax of the Festival came with the performance of *The Kingdom* on the Thursday morning, with as fine a quartet of soloists as could be found in England at that time. A wonderfully expressive description of the occasion by Wulstan Atkins[133] says everything:

I can see it again today: Elgar conducting, with Elsie Suddaby, Astra Desmond, Frank Titterton and Harold Williams around, him and Billy leading the orchestra, and the chorus and orchestra following his every movement and quietly and surely meeting his every wish. Elgar's movements were slight and less demonstrative than they would have been years before, and at times it was as if he was himself being carried away by his own music. But the performance was perfect and strangely intimate and reflective. Perhaps memories were passing through his mind of his writing this work in Hereford twenty-seven years before, or more likely later events have added poignancy to my own memories. Elsie Suddaby's singing of 'The sun goeth down', and the last chorus, 'Thou, O Lord God, art our Father, and we are Thine', with Elgar very quietly putting down his stick after the last chord had faded away, will always remain in my memory.

Edward Elgar had laid down his baton for the last time; the Three Choirs Festival had bidden him farewell. Five months later, after much suffering, he died at his home overlooking the Cathedral that he loved so much, and to which he had given so much through his music.

5

Coda

'It is hardly too much to say that he who has not heard Elgar's music at these Festivals only half knows what Elgar is. Elgar is a romantic spirit, the roots of whose being are in the past, in a way that cannot be felt everywhere as it is here. Worcester, the faithful city, is faithful enough to the association in which his music is born to give it a setting that takes the imagination back far enough to feel whence its strength has come. The very walls cry out to us from the same romantic past that has bred his music. His music, heard within them, is redolent of England in the complete sense which in other places may fail it.'[134]

No more poetic words have ever been written about Elgar and his musical relationship with the Three Choirs Festival. With their icon having gone, how would the festivals now face the future?

As the end of 1933 approached it was clear to Sumsion and his committee that, even if he survived that long, the master would not be able to take an active part in their forthcoming festival. Three of Elgar's major works were programmed at Gloucester - *The Kingdom*, the *Second*

Symphony and *The Dream of Gerontius*. With the composer's death Sumsion decided that it would be right and proper for the conducting of his works to be shared between the three 'organists'. Sumsion himself directed *The Kingdom* (designated as the memorial performance in the programme), while Hull conducted the *Symphony*, and Atkins took charge of *The Dream of Gerontius*. This sharing of work not only released the host conductor from the responsibility of taking over the huge burden of conducting that was created by Elgar's absence, but it was also the incentive for establishing a pattern of conducting responsibilities which still holds to this day.

Sumsion frequently referred to the extraordinary feelings of emotion and grief shared between performers and audiences at that festival. A feeling of intense sadness dominated the whole week, and it became extremely difficult to develop any sort of festive atmosphere; not surprisingly the performances themselves had a very special sensitivity of the sort that would never be experienced again. The spirit of commemoration would inevitably carry over to Worcester for the following year when there were performances of *The Apostles*, the *'Cello Concerto*, the *Introduction and Allegro*, a couple of works at the Opening Service, and the commemorative performance of *The Dream of Gerontius*, which had followed the unveiling of the Elgar Memorial Window in the north aisle of the Cathedral – above the composer's favourite spot for listening to so many performances of his own music at the festivals. The ceremony was conducted with a sense of pageantry which would have warmed Elgar's heart, and the performance of the oratorio which followed was considered to be finer than any that had been heard in those hallowed surroundings. It was indeed the most appropriate farewell that could ever be imagined.

In each of the three festivals that preceded the second cessation of activities in the century, Elgar was represented by no less than four major works, together with the usual representative pieces at the Opening Service and, at the Hereford revival of 1946, there was once more again a veritable feast of his music. The excitement that surrounded the performance of *The Kingdom* at the first concert of that festival will live long in the memory of those who were privileged to be there; the 'old festival' was on the road again, and the glorious music of Elgar seemed a perfect vehicle to set it on its way.

Festival conductors came and went for the remaining fifty years of the century, but the music of Elgar always figured prominently in the programmes, even if representation was rather sparse on occasions during the late 1950s and early 1960s, when his music went out of fashion. Some interesting points emerge from this period: Worcester 1948 witnessed the first appearance of Kathleen Ferrier at the festival with her sensational singing in *The Dream of Gerontius*; the *Enigma Variations* were played in the cathedral for the first time at Hereford in 1949, for, prior to that, the work had always been presented in a 'secular' venue; *The Dream of Gerontius* was given at the final concert of a festival for the first time at Hereford in 1955, a position it has occupied in the programme on several occasions since; Walton's *Belshazzar's Feast* was finally admitted into the Three Choirs repertoire at Worcester in 1957, prefaced by Elgar's *Introduction and Allegro*; the start of *The Dream of Gerontius* at Hereford in 1967 was delayed by a bomb hoax, and, as has already been mentioned, *The Apostles* and *The Kingdom* were performed on the same day at Worcester in 1984, a unique happening in the history of the Festival, and one that proved to be wholly satisfying and illuminating - if both physically and emotionally exhausting!

It follows then that the new millennium will find Elgar firmly established as an essential feature in the scenario of the Three Choirs Festival. He had relied on the Three Choirs to give him an airing and, although it took a while for the hierarchy to recognise his potential, his first commission (*Froissart*) was interesting in that it explored his skills as an orchestrator rather than following the predicable line of a cantata, for we should remember that, in the nineteenth century, the outlets for a young composer to display his talents were almost exclusively restricted to choral festivals, of which the Three Choirs was the flagship. Whereas on the continent a composer would announce his arrival with a symphony or an opera, in England it was necessary to produce a successful piece for one of the multitude of choral groups, or for one of the provincial choral festivals. In a sense Elgar was following the only course available to him in accepting the 1890 commission, but, in doing so, he sounded an original and personal note, and the fact that his first composition for this traditional choral event was an orchestral work is significant in itself.

After the success of *Froissart*, Elgar was to grace the portals of this celebrated event for over forty years as composer, conductor, advisor, listener, socialite and celebrity. Without his presence and his music the Three Choirs Festival would almost certainly have become a very different event during the course of the century. A festival of this sort needed a figure of Elgar's stature on which to hang its raison d'être, and the fact that he was a son of its own milieu was an added bonus.

It would be unnatural to expect all the performances he directed to have been impeccable. In Elgar's music the festival chorus were faced with demands which were outside the normal expectancy of the British choral tradition: balance of parts, awareness of harmonic implications, the importance of individual melodic lines often demanding previously unexplored vocal mannerisms, and a new principle of tone quality and sonority – all were contrary to the conventional paths of choralism. Then there was the fact that the dramatic content of the cantatas and oratorios of the nineteenth century had been superseded by a new blend of mysticism and contemplation; this was an even greater challenge to master for those brought up on an endless round of Mendelssohn and his imitators. The movement against the *Elijah* syndrome, which had maintained such a hold over this country's choral activities, reached its conclusion with the advent of *The Dream of Gerontius*. It could hardly be expected that the Three Choirs would immediately take this revolution on board, and there were also other factors to work against it, such as lack of rehearsal time, as well as Elgar's idiosyncratic approach to his own music when on the podium; but when the inspiration really flowed the results were magical, and by all accounts there were plenty of those special occasions to cherish. As Michael Kennedy has written:

> . . . in those works which he conducted so magnificently his spirit lives in a thousand allusions and associations.[135]

Elgar's orchestral masterpieces now readily take their rightful place alongside those of the great masters in musical history, and it cannot be envisaged that the Three Choirs will ever forsake them. Of course the same is true of *The Dream of Gerontius*, and it is surely a responsibility of Three Choirs to ensure regular airings of those incomparable oratorios, *The Apostles* and *The Kingdom*. There is little doubt that both are handicapped by comparison with the near-perfection of *Gerontius*. Certainly they may be more difficult to grasp, not least because, at first sight, they appear to lack a certain unity and spontaneity, but both oratorios express a deep underlying mysticism and, in a way, are a continuation of the Passions of J.S. Bach and others. The extraordinary sequence of texts, which Elgar himself selected, show a profound knowledge of the Bible, as well as bearing some comparisons with the compilation that Jennens produced for Handel in the *Messiah*, drawing from the composer some intensely moving passages. This is music which can be safely and ideally appreciated and preserved in the framework of the Three Choirs, even if the rest of the musical world puts them into the category of being merely historically interesting and representing the end of a particular form of musical expression. Hopefully the future choralists will also continue to look favourably on *The Music Makers*.

During the next decade or so we shall be passing through a series of important centenary milestones in Elgar's creative output, and the response of the Three Choirs will be eagerly anticipated. Atkins, Hull and Sumsion all continued the direct influence of the composer after his death, and they all laid down the pattern of 'Elgar performances' for the future; it is essential that this tradition is religiously maintained, for it is here at this truly English festival that the genuine influence of a great English composer can be most felt. As Reginald Nettel wrote in reference to Elgar's participation in concerts at North Staffordshire:

> Elgar was the last of the great British musicians to spring from the common people. His successors have all sprung from artistic circles, with an outlook original and sincere enough, but not always to be loved with the same simple affection.[136]

The repertoire statistics at the end of this study prove only too well how Elgar's music has taken its rightful place in the festival programmes beside Bach, Beethoven, Handel, Mozart and the whole range of the great names in musical history; the fact that he did spring from the 'common people' of this incomparable tradition makes his role in the festival's history unique. Bayreuth without Wagner and Salzburg without Mozart would be unthinkable; surely the Three Choirs Festival and Elgar are just as inseparable.

'. . . on one man's soul it hath broken,
a light that doth not depart;
and his look, or a word he hath spoken,
wrought flame in another man's heart.'

Notes

[1] at the 1881 Festival.

[2] *'A Future for English Music' and other lectures by Edward Elgar*, edited by Percy M. Young, 1968.

[3] W.H.Elgar (1822-1906) was organist at St George's Roman Catholic Church in Worcester from 1846 to 1885.

[4] except Hereford 1852.

[5] Organist of Gloucester Cathedral from 1865 to his death in 1876; he conducted four Gloucester Festivals.

[6] from an article in *The Strand Magazine*, 1904.

[7] *The Three Pears* annual magazine, 1931.

[8] *Edward Elgar: the record of a friendship* by Rosa Burley, referring to a Bavarian holiday in 1893.

[9] Until 1954 the audience seats ran from east to west, in order to avoid a supposed lack of respect to the altar.

[10] *The Three Pears* annual magazine, 1931.

[11] *Origins and Progress of the Meeting of the Three Choirs*, 1895.

[12] Letter to his friend Dr C.W. Buck (1852-1932) of Giggleswick in Yorkshire, 28th September, 1884.

[13] *Musical Times*, 1884.

[14] For much of the nineteenth century the Festival chorus was augmented by singers from various centres, the chief sources of supply coming from Leeds, Lichfield, Birmingham, Oxford and Cardiff, as well as some professional stiffening from London. This practice was eventually phased out at the turn of the century: Worcester was the last to abandon it in 1902.

[15] The original manuscript of the *Overture 'Froissart'* is in the possession of the Elgar Birthplace Museum at Broadheath.

[16] *The Origins and Progress of the Meeting of the Three Choirs*, 1895.

[17] *The Elgar-Atkins Friendship* by E. Wulstan Atkins, 1984.

[18] *The Black Knight* was first performed in the Public Hall, Worcester, on 18th April, 1893, conducted by the composer. It received its first Three Choirs performance on 22nd August, 1984.

[19] The North Staffordshire Musical Festival is being revived in October 1999, marking the centenary of the demise of this famous event.

[20] The Elgars attended this first performance - the earliest evidence of their attendance at an 'away' festival as listeners.

[21] The *Serenade* was first played privately in Worcester at some undated occasion during 1892, but had to wait until 1899 before it received its first public performance in England - at New Brighton, conducted by the composer.

[22] Elgar's note on the copy of the Festival programme, in the possession of the Elgar Birthplace Museum.

[23] Surprisingly dedicated to Dr C. Swinnerton Heap, also the dedicatee of *The Light of Life*.

[24] Dr C.W. Buck.

[25] The *Requiem* was included in the programme for 1896 - a first time at the Three Choirs Festival - presumably as a result of some persuasion from Elgar.

[26] The manuscript of the full score is in the possession of the Elgar Birthplace Museum at Broadheath.

[27] Elgar had ordered a bell-tent to be set up in his garden at 'Forli' in Malvern Link, where he could enjoy the fine summer weather and carry on his work uninterrupted. A raised flag was the warning not to be disturbed. The scores of the two 1896 works were mostly conceived under this canvas shelter.

[28] *Sir Edward Elgar*, by R.J. Buckley, 1912.

[29] 7th September, 1896.

[30] Alberto Randegger (1832-1911), Italian-born singer teacher, conductor and composer, who settled in London in 1855, becoming conductor of the Carl Rosa Opera and Director of the Norwich Festival.

[31] The Revd. Edward Vine Hall, himself a composer and conductor, who had given the first performance of Elgar's *Serenade for Strings*.

[32] October, 1986.

[33] 15th September, 1896.

[34] 31st October, 1896.

[35] *The Light of Life* was performed on 18th August, 1996, at the Three Choirs Festival, with Alison Pearce, Margaret McDonald, Neil Jenkins, Robert Hayward, and the Royal Liverpool Philharmonic Orchestra, conducted by Donald Hunt.

King Olaf was performed in the Victoria Hall, Hanley, on 21st October, 1996, with Susan Chilcott, Arthur Davies, Alan Opie, the Ceramic City Choir and the BBC Philharmonic, conducted by Donald Hunt.

[36] Worcester Festival programme note, 1996.

[37] from a letter to A J. Jaeger, December 1898.

[38] Horatio W. Parker (1863-1919), director of music at Holy Trinity, Boston, and Professor of Music at Yale University from 1894; the first American to have works performed at the Three Choirs Festival - Worcester, 1899 and 1902, Hereford 1900.

[39] from a letter to A.J. Jaeger, February 1898.

[40] Born in Llandaff, Atkins moved to Worcester from Ludlow Parish Church, where he had been organist and choirmaster since 1893, having previously been Sinclair's assistant at both Truro and Hereford Cathedrals. He remained at Worcester until 1950, having been in charge of no less than fifteen festivals. He was knighted in 1921.

[41] A local man of exceptional talent but limited experience, Brewer succeeded Charles Lee Williams (1853-1935) in 1897, conducting eight festivals at Gloucester. He was knighted shortly before his sudden death in March, 1928, six months before the Gloucester Festival, which he had planned.

[42] Born in Hereford, where he was a cathedral chorister and articled pupil/assistant to Sinclair, he was appointed organist and master of the choristers at Hereford Cathedral after his return from the war in 1918, holding the post until 1949. He was chief conductor at eight festivals, and was knighted in 1947.

[43] *Elgar at Hereford*, by P. C. Hull, in the Royal Academy of Music magazine, 1960.

[44] Born in Düsseldorf, Jaeger took up residence in England when he was eighteen, and joined the staff of Novello in 1890, becoming a publishing adviser to the firm. He was quick to recognise Elgar's potential, becoming the composer's close friend and mentor until his untimely death from tuberculosis in 1909.

[45] from a letter to A.J. Jaeger, August 1897.

[46] from a letter to Edward Elgar, September 1897.

[47] Nicholas Kilburn (1843-1923) was an accomplished musician, educated at Cambridge and Durham universities, obtaining a doctorate from the latter, although by profession he was an iron merchant based in Bishop Auckland. He achieved great success as a

conductor of choral societies in the North, specialising in the works of Elgar, for which he was rewarded by the composer with the dedication of *The Music Makers.*

[48] Miss Ellicott was the daughter of Bishop Ellicott, who served the Gloucester Diocese from 1863 until his death in 1905. He was wholly unmusical and was opposed to the Three Choirs Festival, generally finding himself 'out of town' when the event was being held.

[49] *Memories of Choirs and Cloisters* by A. Herbert Brewer, 1931.

[50] Son of a Sierra Leone physician and English mother, Coleridge-Taylor studied composition with Stanford at the Royal College of Music. He is best known for his *Hiawatha* trilogy, the first part of which also appeared in 1898. Other first performances followed at the Festivals of 1899, 1900, 1901 and 1903, all conducted by the composer, but his music has never been heard at a Three Choirs since.

[51] Sullivan retired from the post after the 1898 Festival due to ill health, and was replaced by Sir Charles Stanford, who remained principal conductor until 1910.

[52] Acworth (1849-1933) had previously helped Elgar to select and 'modify' the text for his cantata *King Olaf.*

[53] 5th October, 1898.

[54] 6th October, 1898.

[55] Scene 3 was included in the secular concert at Hereford in 1900.

[56] The second performance had been conducted by Granville Bantock (1868-1946) at New Brighton.

[57] *The Elgar Atkins Friendship* by E. Wulstan Atkins, 1984.

[58] *Edward Elgar, Memories of a Variation*, 1937.

[59] A copy of the score and a recording of *Hora Novissima* was brought to my attention on a recent visit to Boston with the Cathedral Choir. A revival of this fascinating work would not have come amiss in its Worcester centenary year.

[60] Dvořák ultimately produced a *Requiem* for the Birmingham Festival of 1891. This fine work was given at the 1894 Hereford Festival, and was not repeated until Worcester 1984, conducted in a memorable performance by John Sanders.

[61] First heard publicly in 1896.

[62] Three of the songs were given at the secular concert at Worcester in 1902, and two were heard at the equivalent concert at Worcester in 1911 but, amazingly, the full cycle was not presented at a Festival until Gloucester in 1983.

[63] from *Allgemeine Musik Zeitung*, translated for the *Musical Times*, January 1901.

[64] Elgar completed his Concert Overture earlier in the year, and gave its première in London on 20 June, 1901.

[65] 4th November, 1900.

[66] Bennett had been principal music critic of *The Daily Telegraph* for many years. He had already compiled texts for works such as Sullivan's *The Golden Legend* and Cowen's *Ruth,* both of which had been performed at a Three Choirs Festival. Elgar briefly corresponded with Bennett regarding a libretto for the abandoned oratorio on the life of Saint Augustine.

[67] The full account of this collaboration and the legal problems surrounding the libretto are included in Brewer's *Memories of Choirs and Cloisters.*

[68] The revival of *Emmaus* was conducted by John Sanders, with soloists Alison Hargan, Margaret Cable, John Mitchinson, Mark Wildman, and accompanied by the Royal Liverpool Philharmonic Orchestra.

[69] *The Elgar-Atkins Friendship*, by Wulstan Atkins, 1984.

[70] A son of the Archbishop of Canterbury, Benson was an assistant master at Eton, and was well-known in royal circles. Elgar later used some of Benson's verse for three of his solo songs, but their greatest collaboration will for ever be seen (or rather, heard) as *Land of Hope and Glory*, the final section of the *Coronation Ode*.

[71] Friday, 24th August: Lillian Watson, Sally Burgess, Maldwyn Davies, Peter Savidge, with the BBC Philharmonic, conducted by Donald Hunt.

[72] Although a cotton broker by profession Rodewald was something of an impressario in the Liverpool musical scene, and was much respected as a conductor by both Dr Richter and Elgar, who became a close friend and dedicatee of the first *Pomp and Circumstance March in D.*

[73] *Strand Magazine*, May 1904.

[74] extract from a letter to Ivor Atkins dated 31st August, 1902.

[75] Began his career as music director at New Brighton, where he was responsible for promoting the works of contemporary British composers, including Elgar. Bantock, himself a prolific composer in the high romantic style, became Principal of the Birmingham School of Music in 1900, succeeding Elgar as Professor of Music, Birmingham University in 1908. He was knighted in 1930.

[76] extracts from a letter to the music critic and author, Ernest Newman (1868-1959), 11th September, 1902.

[77] William Henry Reed (1876-1942), violinist, composer, teacher and author, who led the London Symphony Orchestra from 1912-1935. His memorial tablet in Worcester Cathedral is situated appropriately below the Elgar memorial window.

[78] Francis Howard Lee Schuster (1857-1927), a wealthy patron of the arts who, with his sister Adele, developed a close friendship with the Elgars.

[79] from *Annals of the Three Choirs - continuation of history and progress* by Lee Williams, Chance and Hannam-Clark, 1931.

[80] *The Daily Telegraph*, 15 October, 1903.

[81] Hungarian-born, Richter was Wagner's assistant at Bayreuth, before settling in London in 1877. He was conductor of the Hallé Orchestra from 1900 to 1911, and chief conductor at several festivals. He was the dedicatee of Elgar's *First Symphony*.

[82] *In the South* had been completed earlier in the year, and received its first performance at the London Elgar Festival on 16th March.

[83] Lloyd was at Gloucester from 1876 to 1882; his subsequent appointments were to Christ Church, Oxford, Eton College and the Chapel Royal. A composer of modest attainment, he was highly regarded for a time in church circles.

[84] extract from *The Kingdom - analytical & descriptive notes*, by A.J. Jaeger, 1906.

[85] Both reviews appeared on 4th October, 1906.

[86] Italian-born violinist and music critic, who became a member of the Hallé Orchestra under Richter, at the same time writing for the *Manchester Guardian*. He later became the critic for *The Daily Telegraph*.

[87] extract from an essay *Elgar* in *The Music Masters*, edited by A.L. Bacharach.

[88] *Yorkshire Post*, 9th September 1908.

[89] from *Elgar as I knew him*, by W.H. Reed, 1937.

[90] Fritz Kreisler (1875-1962), Austrian-born violinist and composer, whose brilliant technique and unique quality of tone placed him in the forefront of international virtuosi. He appeared regularly in Britain, giving the first performance of Elgar's *Violin Concerto* in London on 10th November, 1910.

[91] from *Elgar as I knew him*, by W.H. Reed, 1937.

[92] Until the mid-1950s the Morning Concert consisted of two sessions, with a lunch break.

[93] *The Birmingham Gazette*, 15th September, 1911.

94 A full explanation of the various allusions can be found in *The Elgar-Atkins Friendship*, by E. Wulstan Atkins.

95 Wife of Charles Stuart-Wortley, member of parliament for Sheffield, who was made a baron in 1916. The families had met at the 1902 Sheffield Festival, becoming close friends. Alice (1862-1936), the daughter of Millais, the pre-Raphaelite painter, was Elgar's 'Windflower', and she became enshrined in his *Violin Concerto*.

96 The Royal Philharmonic Orchestra, conducted by Vernon Handley.

97 Embleton was an exceedingly rich man who lavished his generosity on the Leeds Choral Union. The Elgars invariably received hospitality from Embleton on their frequent visits to Leeds.

98 A setting of Psalm 29, written for the Festival of the Sons of the Clergy in St Paul's Cathedral, London, on 30th April, 1914.

99 extract from a letter date 2nd July, 1914, quoted in *The Elgar-Atkins Friendship*, by E. Wulstan Atkins.

100 extract from a letter to Alice Stuart-Wortley, September 1917.

101 May 6th, 1920.

102 from *Annals of the Three Choirs - a continuation of history and progress* by Lee Williams, Chance and Hannam-Clark, 1931.

103 The complete work was not heard at a Three Choirs Festival until Worcester 1993, when it was conducted by John Sanders, with Julie Kennard and the Royal Liverpool Philharmonic Orchestra.

104 Alexander Brent Smith (1889-1950), educated at the King's School, Worcester, was director of music at Lancing College from 1913-34. He was a respected author and composer in his time, his finest work being the *Elegy* composed in memory of Elgar, and first performed at Hereford in 1946.

105 Julius Harrison (1885-1963) was born at Stourport. He became a noted orchestral conductor in the 1920s and 30s, making a special feature of English music. A specialist in the music of Brahms, he wrote several books, and in later life concentrated on composition - the most important being the *Mass in C* and a *Requiem* (first performed at Worcester 1957).

106 In the letter to Atkins, quoted previously, Elgar had written: 'The Messiah you know I love and am delighted it is in its old place.'

107 A fifteenth century cottage in the heart of the Sussex countryside where the Elgars

lived from May 1917. Edward moved back to London in August 1921, after months of trying to come to terms with life at Brinkwells without Alice.

[108] The first Three Choirs performances of these works were as follows: the *Violin Sonata* - Worcester 1975; the *String Quartet* - Worcester 1978; the *Piano Quintet* - Hereford 1921.

[109] Extract from an interview with Olin Downes in the *New York Times* early in 1930.

[110] 2 November 1919.

[111] Organist of Christ Church Cathedral, Oxford, 1909-26, and Precentor of Eton College, 1926-45.

[112] First performed at a Philharmonic concert at the Queen's Hall, London in March 1920.

[113] extract from a letter to Herbert Brewer.

[114] a quote from *As I remember* by Arthur Bliss, 1970.

[115] Sir Walter Parratt (1841-1924), organist and composer, who was Master of the Queen's (King's) Musick from 1893 until his death.

[116] Sir Frederick Bridge (1844-1924), a Worcestershire-born organist and conductor who was organist of Westminster Abbey 1882-1918, and conductor of the Royal Choral Society 1896-1922.

[117] A Gloucestershire author and composer, mainly of songs.

[118] *Elgar and the Public,* an article from the *Musical Times*, January 1931.

[119] *Annals of the Three Choirs*, 1931.

[120] Ibid.

[121] extracts from a letter to Ivor Atkins, February 2nd, 1926.

[122] extract from a letter to the *Worcester Daily Times*, 17th March 1926.

[123] extract from a letter to Ivor Atkins, 29th September 1926.

[124] The American, Frederick Gaisberg (1873-1951), came to England to record for HMV, having had previous experience at home with the Columbia Phonograph Company. He became Recording Artists Manager, especially favouring the music of Elgar, of whom he became a close friend in the composer's final years.

[125] 6th December 1928.

[126] 9th January 1929.

[127] George Bernard Shaw (1856-1950), music critic and playwright, who became a

significant inspiration to Elgar in his last years, encouraging him to work at an opera and the *Third Symphony*.

[128] *The Birmingham Post*, 10th September, 1931.

[129] extract from a letter to the Elgar Society Newsletter, May 1975.

[130] from a letter dated 28th June 1932.

[131] from Elgar in the Penguin *Lives of Great Composers*, 1935.

[132] from the *Elgar-Atkins Friendship* by E. Wulstan Atkins.

[133] Ibid.

[134] Samuel Langford, writing in the *Manchester Guardian*, 1924.

[135] *Elgar and the Festivals* from *The Two Hundred and Fifty Years of the Three Choirs Festival*, 1977.

[136] from *Music in the Five Towns 1840-1914*, 1944.

Elgar at the Three Choirs Festival - Repertoire 1890-1999

> Dates which are asterisked indicate that Elgar conducted the work on that occasion; the letter prefix refers to the place where the Festival was held.

Choral:

The Dream of Gerontius G1901* (Prelude and Angel's Farewell); W1902*;
H1903*; G1904* (Prelude and Angel's Farewell);
W1905; H1906; W1908; G1910*; H1912*;
G1913*; W1920; H1921*; W1923*; H1924*;
H1927*; G1928*; W1929*; H1930*; G1931*;
W1932*; H1933*; G1934; W1935; H1936;
G1937;W1938; H1946; G1947; W1948; H1949;
G1950; W1951; H1952; G1953; W1954; H1955;
G1956; W1957; H1958; G1959; W1960; H1961;
G1962; W1963; H1964; G1965; W1966; H1967;
G1968; W1969; H1970; G1971; W1975; H1976;
G1977; W1978; H1979; W1984; H1985; W1987;
W1990; G1992; H1994; W1996.

The Apostles G1904*; W1905*; H1906; G1907*; H1909;
H1921*; G1922*; G1925*; W1926*;
H1927(Prologue); H1930*; W1935; H1936;
G1947; H1949 (Prologue); W1954; W1957
(Prologue); W1963 (Prologue); H1973; W1981;
W1984; G1995.

The Kingdom	G1907*; W1908*; G1922*; W1923*; H1924*; W1926*; H1927*;G1928*; W1929*; H1933*; G1934; H1946; W1948; W1949; W1951; H1958; W1960 (Prelude); H1964 ;W1966 (Prelude); H1970; G1980; W1984; G1989; G1995; W1999.
The Light of Life	W1896*; G1898* (Meditation); W1899*; W1975 (Meditation); W1996.
The Music Makers	W1920*; H1927*; W1932*; W1938; W1975; G1983; H1988; G1998.
Caractacus	H1900 (Scene3); H1933 (March);W1972 (March); G1977; H1979 (March); G1989; H1994 (March).
For the Fallen	W1920*; G1922*; W1923*; G1925*; W1926*; W1932*; H1946.
The Spirit of England	W1993.
The Black Knight	W1984.
Coronation Ode	W1990.
Te Deum	H1897*; H1900; H1903; H1909; H1985; H1994.
Benedictus	H1897*; H1900; H1994.
Give unto the Lord	H1967; H1973; W1978 ; H1982; H1991; W1996.
Great is the Lord	W1984; W1990.
Go, song of mine	H1909*; W1911; H1924; W1984; G1989; G1995.
Partsongs, Op 53	H1982; W1984.
Weary wind of the West	W1972.
Evening Scene	W1972.
O happy eyes	W1972.
Feasting I watch	W1990.
The Wanderer	W1990.
The Snow	W1981; H1982.

Fly, singing-bird, fly	W1981; H1982.
Christmas Greeting	H1982.
Ave verum corpus	W1972.
Chants	W1984.
Hymn: Drake's Broughton	G1995.

Vocal:

Like to the damask rose	W1978.
Pleading	G1992.
Queen Mary's Song	W1978.
Sea Pictures	W1902 (songs 2 ,4 & 5); W1911 (songs 1 & 3); G1983; H1991.
Shakespeare's Kingdom	G1992.
Speak, music	W1935; W1978; G1992.
The River	H1912*.
The Shepherd's Song	W1978; G1992.
The Torch	H1912*.

Orchestral:

Symphony No 1	H1909*; G1910*; G1925*; H1930*; W1932*; G1956; G1965; H1973; H1979; W1987; W1996.
Symphony No 2	W1911*; G1913*; H1927*; W1929*; G1934; W1951; W1957 (4th movement); W1972; W1978; G1986; W1990; H1997.
Violin Concerto	W1911*; H1927*; G1931*; H1936; W1938; W1951; H1961; W1969; G1977; W1981; H1988; W1993; G1998.

'Cello Concerto	H1921*; W1923*; H1924*; G1928*; W1935; G1937; G1950; G1959; W1966; H1976; G1980; W1984; H1988.
Overture Cockaigne	G1901*;W1902*; H1909*; H1927; H1936; H1985; W1987 (Band); W1993.
Overture Froissart	W1890*; W1984; W1990; H1994.
Overture In the South	G1904; H1930; W1948; W1987; G1992.
Enigma Variations	W1899*; H1903*; W1926*; W1938; H1946; H1949; H1952; W1957; H1976; W1987; H1991; W1999.
Introduction and Allegro	W1905*; H1906*; W1920*; H1924*; W1929*; H1930*; W1935; G1937; H1946; G1953; W1957; G1971; W1975; H1979; H1985; G1986; W1993.
Serenade for Strings	G1950; H1970; G1977; W1978; G1983; G1986; W1987; G1998.
Coronation March, 1911	W1911*; H1912; G1913; W1975.
Dream Children	W1926; W1978; W1981 (Piano).
Crown of India Suite	H1912*.
Nursery Suite	G1931*.
Severn Suite	W1932 (Orch)*; W1978 (Brass); G1986 (Brass); W1990 (Brass).
Wand of Youth Suite No 2	W1908*.
Elegy	W1960; W1963; G1974.
Civic Fanfare	H1930*; H1933; H1936; G1937; H1946; H1949; H1973.
Pomp and Circumstance 1	W1981.
Pomp and Circumstance 4	H1958.

Pomp and Circumstance 5	W1969; H1973; H1985.
Imperial March	H1897; W1963; G1971; W1975; G1977; H1979; H1985; H1988; H1991.
Three Characteristic Pieces	W1978.
Suite: The Starlight Express	W1978.
Chanson de Matin	W1978; W1984.
Chanson de Nuit	W1978; W1984.
Sursum Corda	W1902; W1920; W1963; W1984; H1985; H1994.
Suite: From the Bavarian Highlands	W1984; W1987 (Band).
Falstaff	G1989.
Empire March	H1924.

Chamber and Instrumental:

String Quartet	W1978; W1984; W1990; W1993; W1996; G1998; W1999.
Piano Quintet	H1921; W1932; W1981; W1996.
Violin Sonata	W1975; W1987; H1994.
Romance	W1978.
Skizze	W1981.
In Smyrna	W1981; H1991.
Organ Sonata	G1937 (1st movement); H1952; W1957; W1960; W1966; W1972; G1974 (1st movement); H1982; W1984 (1st movement); H1985 (1st movement); G1989 (3rd & 4th movements); W1999.
Vesper Voluntaries	W1990; W1996.

Arrangements by Elgar:

arr. National Anthem	Used regularly from 1902 until 1974 (for some years the version of the National Anthem is not specified), then H1976; G1977; H1979; W1984; H1985; H1988; H1991; H1994; H1997.
arr. Fantasia and Fugue in c – Bach	G1922; G1928*; W1929; W1981; W1990; W1996.
arr. Overture in d – Handel	W1923; H1924; W1926; G1931; W1935; W1948; G1950; W1954; G1965; H1979; H1991.
orch. Abide with me – Atkins	W1923.
orch. Advent Cantata – Blair	W1896.
orch. Deborah and Barak – Blair	W1902.
orch. Emmaus – Brewer	G1901; G1907; G1992.
orch. Jehova, quam multi sunt – Purcell	W1929.
orch. Jerusalem – Parry	W1923; G1989; W1996.
orch., Let us lift up our hearts – S.S. Wesley	W1923.
orch. O Lord, look down – Battishill	W1923; H1924; W1926.

Arrangements of Elgar's works:

'Cello Concerto – arr. Lionel Tertis	H1933*.
Enigma Variations – arr. Eric Ball	W1984.
Fragments of Elgar – arr. Robert Walker	W1999.
Imperial March – arr. George Martin	W1990.
March in D – arr. Donald Hunt	W1990.
Organ Sonata – arr. Gordon Jacob	H1991.
Organ Sonata No 2 – arr. Ivor Atkins	H1988; W1996.
Triumphal March (Caractacus) – arr. Edwin Lemare	G1995.

Lectures:

A boy calls from the reeds on Severnside	W1993.
Elgar's Oratorios	W1984.
Elgar of Worcester	W1981.
My Friends Pictured Within	W1990; G1992.
Newman, Elgar, and the Dream of Gerontius	W1990.
Not only Nimrod: but also . . .	W1999.
The Elgar/Atkins Friendship	W1990.
Wood Magic	W1987.

Bibliography

Origin and Progress of the Meeting of the Three Choirs, by Lysons and Amott, continued by C. Lee Williams and H. Godwin Chance. Chance and Bland, 1895.

Annals of the Three Choirs – continuation and progress from 1895 to 1930, by C. Lee Williams, H. Godwin Chance and T. Hannam-Clark. Minchin & Gibbs, 1931.

The Elgar-Atkins Friendship, by E. Wulstan Atkins. David & Charles, 1984.

Three Choirs – A History of the Festival, by Anthony Boden. Alan Sutton, 1992.

Memories of Choirs and Cloisters, by A. Herbert Brewer. Bodley Head, 1931.

Portrait of Elgar, by Michael Kennedy. OUP, 1987.

Elgar and the Festivals, by Michael Kennedy. Three Choirs Festival Association, 1977.

Edward Elgar – A Creative Life, by Jerrold Northrop Moore. OUP, 1987.

Elgar on Record, by Jerrold Northrop Moore. EMI, 1974.

Edward Elgar - Memories of a Variation, by Mrs Richard Powell. OUP, 1937; reissued Methuen, 1949.

An Elgar Companion, edited by Christopher Redwood. Moorland Publishing, 1982.

Elgar as I knew him, by W.H. Reed. Gollanz, 1936; reissued OUP,1989.

The Three Choirs Festival, by Watkins Shaw. Bayliss, 1954.

Three Choirs Festival Book Programmes from 1857 to 1998.

Other sources include various newspaper cuttings, magazine articles, and letters, referred to in the footnotes to the text.